Easy Guide: Certified Information Systems Security Professional (CISSP)

Austin Vern Songer

CONTENTS

Domain 1 – Security Management Practices

The Big Three - C. I. A.
- Confidentiality – Prevent disclosure of data
- Integrity – Prevent modification of data
- Availability – Ensure reliable timely access to data

Other Important Concepts
- Identification – Means in which user claims Identity
- Authentication – Establishes the users Identity
- Accountability – Systems ability to determine actions of users
- Authorization – rights and permissions granted to an individual
- Privacy – Level of confidentiality that a user is given

Objective of Security is to reduce effects of threats and vulnerabilities to a tolerable level.

Risk Analysis
Assess the following:
- Impact of the threat
- Risk of the threat occurring (likelihood)

Controls reduce both the impact of the threat and the likelihood of the threat, important in cost benefit of controls.

Data Classification
- Data classification has high level enterprise wide benefit
- Demonstrates organizations commitment to security
- Helps identify sensitive and vital information
- Supports C.I.A.
- May be required for legal regulatory reasons

Data owners are responsible for defining the sensitivity level of the data.

Government Classification Terms:
- Unclassified – Neither sensitive nor classified, public release is acceptable
- Sensitive But Unclassified (SBU) – Minor secret, no serious damage if disclosed
- Confidential – disclosure could cause damage to National Security
- Secret - disclosure could cause serious damage to National Security
- Top Secret – Highest Level - disclosure could cause exponentially grave damage to National Security

In addition must have a Need to Know – just because you have "secret" clearance does not mean all "secret" data just data with a need to know.

Additional Public Classification Terms
- Public – similar to unclassified, should not be disclosed but is not a problem if it is
- Sensitive – data protected from loss of Confidentiality and integrity
- Private – data that is personal in nature and for company use only
- Confidential – very sensitive for internal use only - could seriously negatively impact the company

Classification Criteria
- Value - number one criteria, if it is valuable it should be protected
- Age – value of data lowers over time, automatic de-classification
- Useful Life – If the information is made obsolete it can often be de-classified
- Personal Association – If the data contains personal information it should remain classified

Distribution may be required in the event of the following:
- Court Order – may be required by court order
- Government Contracts – government contractors may need to disclose classified information
- Senior Level Approval – senior executives may approve release

Information Classification Roles

Owner
- May be executive or manager
- Owner has final corporate responsibility of the data protection
- Makes determination of classification level
- Reviews classification level regularly for appropriateness
- Delegates responsibility of data protection to the Custodian

Custodian
- Generally IT systems personnel
- Running regular backups and testing recovery
- Performs restoration when required
- Maintains records in accordance with the classification policy

User
- Anyone the routinely uses the data
- Must follow operating procedures
- Must take due care to protect
- Must use computing resources of the company for company purposes only

Policies Standards, Guidelines and Procedures
- Policies are the highest level of documentation
- Standards, Guidelines and Procedures derived from policies
- Should be created first, but are no more important than the rest

Senior Management Statement – general high-level statement
- Acknowledgment of importance of computing resources
- Statement of Support for information security
- Commitment to authorize lower level Standards, Guidelines and Procedures

Regulatory Policies – company is required to implement due to legal or regulatory requirements
- Usually very detailed and specific to the industry of the organization
- Two main purposes
  - To ensure the company is following industry standard procedures
  - To give the company confidence they are following industry standard procedures

Advisory Polices – not mandated but strongly suggested.
- Company wants employees to consider these mandatory.
- Advisory Policies can have exclusions for certain employees or job functions

Informative Policies
- Exist simply to inform the reader
- No implied or specified requirements

Standards, Guidelines and Procedures
- Contain actual detail of the policy
- How the policies should be implemented
- Should be kept separate from one another
  - Different Audiences
  - Security Controls are different for each policy type

- Updating the policy is more manageable

Standards - Specify use of technology in a uniform way, compulsory

Guidelines – similar to standards but not compulsory, more flexible

Procedures – Detailed steps, required, sometimes called "practices", lowest level

Baselines – baselines are similar to standards, standards can be developed after the baseline is established

Roles and Responsibilities
- Senior Management – Has ultimate responsibility for security
- Infosec Officer – Has the functional responsibility for security
- Owner – Determines the data classification
- Custodian - Preserves C.I.A.
- User – Performs in accordance with stated policy
- Auditor – Examines Security

Risk Management
Mitigate (reduce) risk to a level acceptable to the organization.

Identification of Risk
- Actual threat
- Possible consequences
- Probable frequency
- Likely hood of event

Risk Analysis
- Identification of risks
- Benefit - cost justification of counter measures

Risk Analysis Terms
- Asset – Resource, product, data
- Threat – Action with a negative impact
- Vulnerability – Absence of control
- Safeguard – Control or countermeasure

- **Exposure Factor**

% of asset loss caused by threat

- **Single Loss Expectancy (SLE) – Expected financial loss for single event**

SLE = Asset Value x Exposure Factor

- **Annualized Rate of Occurrence (ARO)** – represents estimated frequency in which threat will occur within one year

- **Annualized Loss Expectancy (ALE) – Annually expected financial loss**

ALE = SLE x ARO

Risk Analysis
- Risk analysis is more comprehensive than a Business Impact Analysis
- Quantitative – assigns objective numerical values (dollars)
- Qualitative – more intangible values (data)
- Quantitative is a major project that requires a detailed process plan

Preliminary Security Examination (PSE)
- Often conducted prior to the quantitative analysis.
- PSE helps gather elements that will be needed for actual RA

Risk Analysis Steps
1) Estimate of potential loss
2) Analyze potential threats
3) Define the Annualized Loss Expectancy (ALE)

Categories of Threats
- Data Classification – malicious code or logic
- Information Warfare – technically oriented terrorism
- Personnel – Unauthorized system access
- Application / Operational – ineffective security results in data entry errors
- Criminal – Physical destruction, or vandalism
- Environmental – utility outage, natural disaster
- Computer Infrastructure – Hardware failure, program errors
- Delayed Processing – reduced productivity, delayed collections processing

Annualized Loss Expectancy (ALE)
- Risk analysis should contain the following:
    - Valuation of Critical Assets
    - Detailed listing of significant threats
    - Each threats likelihood
    - Loss potential by threat
    - Recommended remedial safeguards

Remedies
- **Risk Reduction** - implementation of controls to alter risk position
- **Risk Transference** – get insurance, transfer cost of a loss to insurance
- **Risk Acceptance** – Accept the risk, absorb loss

Qualitative Scenario Procedure
- Scenario Oriented
- List the threat and the frequency
- Create exposure rating scale for each scenario
- Scenario written that address each major threat
- Scenario reviewed by business users for reality check
- Risk Analysis team evaluates and recommends safeguards
- Work through each finalized scenario
- Submit findings to management

Value Assessment
- Asset valuation necessary to perform cost/benefit analysis
- Necessary for insurance
- Supports safeguard choices

Safeguard Selection
- Perform cost/benefit analysis
- Costs of safeguards need to be considered including
- Purchase, development and licensing costs
- Installation costs
- Disruption to production
- Normal operating costs

Cost Benefit Analysis
ALE (PreControl) – ALE (PostControl) = Annualized value of the control

Level of manual operations
- The amount of manual intervention required to operate the safeguard
- Should not be too difficult to operate

Auditability and Accountability
Safeguard must allow for auditability and accountability

Recovery Ability
- During and after the reset condition
- No asset destruction during activation or reset
- No covert channel access to or through the control during reset
- No security loss after activation or reset
- Defaults to a state that does not allow access until control are fully operational

Security Awareness Training
Benefits of Awareness
- Measurable reduction in unauthorized access attempts
- Increase effectiveness of control
- Help to avoid fraud and abuse

Periodic awareness sessions for new employees and refresh other

Methods of awareness improvement
- Live interactive presentations
- CBTs
- Publishing of posters and newsletters
- Incentives and awards
- Reminders, login banners

Training & Education
- Security training for Operators
- Technical training
- Infosec training
- Manager training

Domain 2 – Access Control Systems

C - Confidentiality
I - Integrity
A - Availability

Confidentiality
- Not disclosed to unauthorized person

Integrity
- Prevention of modification by unauthorized users
- Prevention of unauthorized changes by otherwise authorized users
- Internal and External Consistency
    - Internal Consistency within the system (i.e. within a database the sum of subtotals is equal to the sum of all units)
    - External Consistency – database with the real world (i.e. database total is equal to the actual inventory in the warehouse)

Availability
- Timely access

Three things to consider
- Threats – potential to cause harm
- Vulnerabilities – weakness that can be exploited
- Risk – potential for harm

Controls
- Preventative – prevent harmful occurrence
- Detective – detect after harmful occurrence
- Corrective – restore after harmful occurrence

Controls can be:
- Administrative – polices and procedures
- Logical or Technical - restricted access
- Physical – locked doors

Three types of access rules:
1. **Mandatory access control (MAC):** Authorization of subject's access to an object depends on labels (sensitivity levels), which indicate subject's clearance, and the classification or sensitivity of the object
    - Every Object is assigned a sensitivity level/label and only users authorized up to that particular level can access the object
    - Access depends on rules and not by the identity of the subjects or objects alone
    - Only administrator (not owners) may change category of a resource — Orange book B-level
    - Output is labeled as to sensitivity level
    - Unlike permission bits or ACLs, labels cannot ordinarily be changed
    - Can't copy a labeled file into another file with a different label
    - Rule based AC

2. **Discretionary Access Control (DAC):** Subject has authority, within certain limits, to specify what objects can be accessible (e.g., use of ACL)
    - User-directed means a user has discretion
    - Identity-based means discretionary access control is based on the subjects identity
    - Very common in commercial context because of flexibility
    - Orange book C level
    - Relies on object owner to control access
    - Identity Based AC

3. **Non-Discretionary Access Control:** Central authority determines what subjects can have access to certain objects based on organization's security policy (good for high turnover)

    - May be based on individual's role in the organization (Role-Based) or the subject's responsibilities or duties (task-based)

Lattice based – provides least access privileges of the access pair
- Greatest lower bound
- Lowest upper bound

	Preventative	Detective
Administrative	Policies and procedures, pre-employment background checks, strict hiring practices, employment agreements, friendly and unfriendly employee termination procedures, vacation scheduling, labeling of sensitive materials, increased supervision, security awareness training, behavior awareness, and sign-up procedures to obtain access to information systems and networks.	Polices and procedures, job rotation, sharing of responsibilities
Technical	Logical system controls, smart cards, bio-metrics, menu shell	IDS, logging, monitoring, clipping levels
Physical	Restrict physical access, guards, man trap, gates	Motion detectors, cameras, thermal detectors

Identification and Authentication
Identification establishes accountability

Three Factor Authentication
- Something you know (password)
- Something you have (token)
- Something you are (biometrics)
Sometimes - something you do

Passwords
- Static – same each time
- Dynamic – changes each time you logon

Tokens – Smartcards
Static Password (like software with pin)
- Owner Authenticates to the token
- Token authenticates to the system

Synchronous Dynamic Password
- Token – generates passcode value
- Pin – user knows
- Token and Pin entered into PC
- Must fit in valid time window

Asynchronous
- Similar to synchronous, new password is generated asynchronously, No time window

Challenge Response
- System generates challenge string
- User enters into token
- Token generates response entered into workstation
- Mechanism in the workstation determines authentication

Biometrics – something you are
- Identify – one to many
- Authenticate – one to one

False Rejection Rate (FRR) – Type I error

False Acceptance Rate (FAR) – Type II error

Crossover Error Rate – (CER) – CER = % when **FRR = FAR**

Biometric Issues
- Enrollment Time – Acceptable rate is **2** minutes per person
- Throughput Time – acceptable rate is **10** people per minute

Acceptability Issues – privacy, physical, psychological

Types of Biometrics
- **Fingerprints**: Are made up of ridge endings and bifurcations exhibited by the friction ridges and other detailed characteristics that are called minutiae.
- **Retina Scans:** Scans the blood-vessel pattern of the retina on the backside of the eyeball.
- **Iris Scans:** Scan the colored portion of the eye that surrounds the pupil.
- **Facial Scans:** Takes attributes and characteristics like bone structures, nose ridges, eye widths, forehead sizes and chin shapes into account.
- **Palm Scans:** The palm has creases, ridges and grooves throughout it that are unique to a specific person.
- **Hand Geometry:** The shape of a person's hand (the length and width of the hand and fingers) measures hand geometry.
- **Voice Print:** Distinguishing differences in people's speech sounds and patterns.
- **Signature Dynamics:** Electrical signals of speed and time that can be captured when a person writes a signature.
- **Keyboard Dynamics:** Captures the electrical signals when a person types a certain phrase.
- **Hand Topology:** Looks at the size and width of an individual's hand and fingers.

Single Sign On
Kerberos
- Symmetric key encryption
- KDC – Kerberos-trusted Key Distribution Center
- TGS – Ticket Granting Service
- AS – Authentication Server

Kerberos
1. KDC knows secret keys of Client and Server
2. KDC exchanges info with the Client and the Server using symmetric keys
3. Using TGS grants temporary symmetric key
4. Client and Server communicate using the temporary session key

Initial Exchange
Client sends Hash Password to the TGS Server, TGS verifies with the Auth. Server
TGS Server responds with:
1) Key for Client and TGS server encrypted with Client Key [K(c,tgs)]Kc

2) Ticket Granting Ticket (TGT) = [K(c, tgs), c,a,v]K(tgs)

Request for Service
Client sends request for service to TGS with
1) TGT = [K(c, tgs), c,a,v]K(tgs)
2) Authenticator K(c, tgs)

TGS Issues Ticket for Service
TGS sends Client back ticket for server and authenticator for server
1) Ticket T(c,s) = [s,c,a,v,K(c,s)]Ks
2) [K(c,s)]K(c,tgs)

Receive Service from Server
Client sends Server
1) Ticket T(c,s) = [s,c,a,v,K(c,s)]Ks
2) authenticator = [c,t,key]K(c,s)

Kerberos weaknesses
- Replay is possible within time frame
- TGS and Auth server are vulnerable as they know everything
- Initial exchange passed on password authentication
- Keys are vulnerable

SESAME – Secure European System for Applications in a Multi-vendor Environment
- Uses Needham-Schroeder protocol
- Uses public key cryptography
- Supports MD5 and CRC32 Hashing
- Uses two tickets
  1) One contains authentication
  2) One contains the access rights to the client

SESAME weaknesses
- Only authenticates by using **first block of message**
- Initial exchange passed on password authentication
- SESAME incorporates two certificates or tickets: One certificate provides authentication as in Kerberos and the other certificate defines the access privileges that are assigned to a client.

KryptoKnight
- Peer to peer relationship between KDC – Key Distribution Center and parties (Client and Server)
- NetSP is based on KryptoKnight
- Supported by RACF
- Authentication
- Key Distribution
- Data Privacy
- Data Integrity
- Single Sign-On
- Administration

Access Control - Centralized and Decentralized
Centralized
- RADIUS - Remote Access Dial-In User Service (incorporates an AS and **dynamic** password)
- TACACS – Terminal Access Controller Access Control System (for network applications, **static** pwd)
- TACACS+ – Terminal Access Controller Access Control System Plus, supports token authentication

CHAP – Challenge Handshake Authentication Protocol
- Supports encryption, protects password

Decentralized
Relational Database Security
- Relational Databases support queries
- Object oriented databases do not support queries

Relational Database
- Data structures called tables (relations)
- Integrity Rules on allowable values
- Operators on the data in tables

Persistency – preservation of integrity through the use of nonvolatile storage media

Schema
- Description of the database
- Defined by Data Description Layer (DDL)

Database Management System (DBMS)
- provides access to the database
- Allows restriction of access

Relational Database
- Relation (table) is the basis of a relational database – relation is represented by a table
- Rows = Records (tuples)
- Column = Attributes

	Attribute-1	Attribute-2	Attribute-3
Record-1			
Record-2			

Primary Key
- Unambiguously identifies a record. Points to a record (tuple)
- Every row (record, tuple) must contain the primary key of the relation (table)

Cardinality - # of rows in a relationship (table)

Degree - # of columns in a relationship (table)

Candidate key - any identifier that is a unique to the record

Foreign Key – any value that matches the primary key of another relation (table)

Relational Database – best suited for text

Relational Database Operations
- **Select** – based on criteria i.e. all items with value > $300.00
- **Join** - join tables based on a common value
- **Union** – forms a new relation (table) from two other relations
- **View** – (virtual table) uses join, project, select - Views can be used to restrict access (least privileges)
- **Query plan**
  - Comprised of implementation procedures, lowest cost plan based on "cost"
  - Costs are CPU time, Disk Access
  - **Bind** – used to create plan

Data Normalization
Ensures that attributes in a table rely only on the primary key

- Eliminates repeating groups
- Eliminates redundant data
- Eliminates attributes not dependent on the primary key

SQL – Structured Query Language
- Select
- Update
- Delete
- Insert
- Grant – Access Privileges
- Revoke – Access Privileges

Object Oriented Databases - OODB
- Best suited for multi-media, graphics
- Steep learning curve
- High overhead

Intrusion Detection
Network Based
- Real Time
- Passive

Host Based
- System and event logs
- Limited by log capabilities

Signature Based – (Knowledge Based)
- Signatures of an attack are stored and referenced
- Failure to recognize slow attacks
- Must have signature stored to identify

Statistical Anomaly Based (Behavior Based)
- IDS determines "normal" usage profile using statistical samples
- Detects anomaly from the normal profile

Access Control Issues
- Confidentiality
- Integrity
- Availability
- Accountability of users

Measures for compensating for both internal and external access violations
- Backups
- RAID – Redundant Array of Inexpensive Disks
- Fault Tolerance
- Business Continuity Planning
- Insurance

Domain 3 – Telecom and Network Security

Management Concepts
Technology Concepts

- Confidentiality – no disclosure of data
- Integrity – no alteration of data
- Availability – no destruction of data

Remote Access Security Management

Remote Connections
- xDSL – Digital Subscriber Line
- Cable modem
- Wireless (PDAs)
- ISDN – Integrated Services Digital Network

Securing External Remote Connections
- VPN – Virtual Private Network
- SSL – Secure Socket Layer
- SSH – Secure Shell

Remote Access Authentication
- RADIUS – Remote Access Dial-In User Server
- TACACS – Terminal Access Controller Access Control Server

Remote Node Authentication
- PAP – Password Authentication Protocol – clear text
- CHAP – Challenge Handshake Authentication Protocol – protects password

Remote User Management
- Justification of remote access
- Support Issues
- Hardware and software distribution

Intrusion Detection
- Notification
- Remediation

Creation of:
- Host and networked based monitoring
- Event Notification
- CIRT – Computer Incident Response Team
    - CIRT Performs
        - Analysis of event
        - Response to incident
        - Escalation path procedures
        - Resolution – post implementation follow up

Intrusion Detection Systems
- **Network Based** – Commonly reside on a discrete network segment and monitor the traffic on that network segment.
- **Host Based** – Use small programs, which reside on a host computer. Detect inappropriate activity only on the host computer, not the network segment.
- **Knowledge Based** – Signature based
- **Behavioral Based** – Statistical Anomaly

Knowledge Based

Pros	Cons
Low false alarms	Resource Intensive
Alarms Standardized	New or unique attacks not found

Behavior Based – less common

Pros	Cons
Dynamically adapts	High False Alarm rates
Not as operating system specific	User activity may not be static enough to implement

CIRT – (CERT) – Computer Incident Response Team

Responsibilities:

- Manage the company's response to events that pose a risk
- Coordinating information
- Mitigating risk, minimize interruptions
- Assembling technical response teams
- Management of logs
- Management of resolution

Network Availability

- RAID – Redundant Array of Inexpensive Disks
- Back Up Concepts
- Manage single points of failure

RAID – Redundant Array of Inexpensive Disks

- Fault tolerance against server crashes
- Secondary – improve system performance
- Striping – Caching and distributing on multiple disks
- RAID employs the technique of striping, which involves partitioning each drive's storage space into units ranging from a sector (512 bytes) up to several megabytes. The stripes of all the disks are interleaved and addressed in order.
- Hardware and software implementation

RAID Advisory Board

- Three types – **Failure Resistant Disk Systems (FRDS)** - the only current standard, Failure Tolerant Disk Systems, and Disaster Tolerant Disk Systems.
- **FRDS**: provides the ability to reconstruct the contents of a failed disk onto a replacement disk.
- Enables the continuous monitoring of these parts and the alerting of their failure
- FRDS+
    - Protect from disk failure – can reconstruct disks by automatically hot swapping while server is running
    - Includes environmental
    - FRDS+ adds hazard warnings

RAID Levels
RAID 0 (STRIPPING)

- Creates one large disk by using multiple disks – striping
- No redundancy
- No fault tolerance (1 fail = all fail)
- Read/Write performance is increased

RAID 1 (MIRRORING)
- Mirroring
- Duplicates data on other disks (usually one to one ratio)
- Expensive (doubles cost of storage)

RAID 2 (HAMMING CODE PARITY)
- Multiple disks
- Parity information created using a hamming code
- Can be used in 39 disk array 32 Data and 7 recovery
- Not used, replaced by more flexible levels

RAID 3 (BYTE LEVEL PARITY) RAID 4 (BLOCK LEVEL PARITY)
- RAID 3 – Byte level
- RAID 4 – Block level
- Stripe across multiple drives
- Parity information on a parity drive
- Provides redundancy
- Can affect performance with single parity drive

RAID 5 (INTERLEAVE PARITY)
- Most popular
- Stripes data and parity information across all drives
- Uses interleave parity
- Reads and writes performed concurrently
- Usually 3-5 drives. If one drive fails, can reconstruct the failed drive by using the information from the other 2.

RAID 7 (SINGLE VIRTUAL DISK)
- Functions as a single virtual disk
- Usually software over Level 5 hardware
- Enables the drive array to continue to operate if any disk or any path to any disk fails.

RAID Summary
0 – Striping
1 – Mirroring
2 – Hamming code parity
3 – Byte level parity
4 – Block level parity
5 – Interleave parity
7 – Single Virtual Disk

Other Types of Fault Tolerance
Redundant Servers
- Primary Server mirrors to secondary server
- Fail-over or rollover to secondary in the event of a failure
- Server fault tolerance can be warm or hot

Server Cluster
- Group of independent servers managed as a single system
- Load Balancing
- Improves performance
- "Server Farm"
- Microsoft Cluster Server

Backup Methodologies

Full Back Up – every file

Incremental
- Only files that have been changed or added recently
- Only files with their archive bit set are backed up.
- This method is fast and uses less tape space but has some inherent vulnerabilities, one being that all incremental backups need to be available and restored from the date of the last full backup to the desired date should a restore be needed.
- Restore = last full backup plus each incremental

Differential
- Only files that have changed since the last backup
- All files to the full backup (additive)
- Restore = full backup plus the last differential

Types of Tape
- DAT – Digital Audio Tape
- QIC – Quarter Inch Cartridge – Small and slow
- 8mm Tape – Superceded by DLT
- DLT – Digital Linear Tape – 4mm tape – large and fast

Other media
CD – permanent backups, longer shelf life than tape
ZIP – JAZZ – Common
Tape Array – 32 to 63 Tape Array using RAID technology
HSM – Hierarchical. Provides a continuous on-line backup by using optical or tape 'jukeboxes', similar to WORMs.

Common Backup Problems
- Slow transfer of data to backup
    - Retrieval time to restore
    - Off hour processing and monitoring
- Server disk space expands over time
- Loss of data between last back up
- Physical security of tapes

Single Points of Failure
Cabling Failures–
- **Coaxial**: many workstations or servers attached to the same segment of cable, which creates a single point of failure if it is broken (similar to cable TV cabling). Exceeding cable length is a source of failure.
- **Twisted Pair**: (CAT3 and CAT 5) The difference between the two has to do with the tightness the copper wires are wound. Tightness determines its resistance to interference. CAT3 is older. Cable length is a common failure
- **Fiber Optic**: Immune to EMI. Longer usable length (upto 2kms). Drawback is costs.

Technology Failures
Ethernet
- Most Popular
- Extremely resistance to failure, especially in a star-wired config.

Token Ring
- Since token is passed by every station on the ring

■ NIC set at wrong speed or in error state can bring the network down

FDDI – Fiber Distributed Data Interface
■ Dual rings fault tolerance (if first ring fails, the secondary ring begins working)
■ Sometimes uses second ring for improved performance

Leased Lines
T1 and ISDN – go with multiple vendors to reduce failures

Frame Relay
■ Public switched WAN
■ Highly Fault Tolerant
■ Bad segment diverts packets
■ Can use multiple vendors for high availability

Other Single Points of Failure
■ Can be any device where all traffic goes through a single device - Router, firewall, hub, switch
■ Power failure – surges, spikes – install UPS

Note: Trivial File Transfer Protocol (TFTP) is good tool for router configuration

Classes of Network Abuse
Class A – unauthorized access through circumvention of security access controls. Masquerading, logon abuse (primarily internal attacks)
Class B – non-business use of systems
Class C – Eavesdropping
■ **Active**: Tampering with a transmission to create a covert signaling channel or probing the network
■ **Passive**: Covertly monitoring or listening to transmissions that is unauthorized.
■ **Covert Channel**: using a hidden unauthorized communication
■ **Tapping:** refers to the physical interception of a transmission medium (like splicing of cable).
Class D – Denial of Service Saturation of network services
Class E – Network Intrusion – penetration (externally)
■ **Spoofing** – A spoofing attack involves nothing more than forging one's source address. It is the act of using one machine to impersonate another.
■ **Piggy Backing** – attack using another users connection
■ **Back Door** – attack via dial up or external connection
Class F – Probing
■ Gives an intruder a road map of the network for DoS attack
■ Gives a list of available services
■ Traffic analysis via 'sniffers' which scans the host for available services
  ■ Like a telephone wiretap allows the FBI to listen in on other people's conversations, a "sniffing" program lets someone listen in on computer conversations.
■ Tools: Telnet (manual), vulnerability scanners (automatic).

Common DoS Attacks
■ Filling hard drive space with email attachments
■ Sending a message that resets a targets host subnet mask causing routing disruption
■ Using up all of the target's resources to accept network connections

Additional DoS Attacks:
Buffer Overflow Attack
■ When a process receives much more data than expected.
■ Since buffers are created to contain a finite amount of data, the extra information - which has to go somewhere - can overflow into adjacent buffers, corrupting or overwriting the valid data held in them.
■ PING – Packet Internet Groper – uses ICMP – Internet Control Message Protocol

■ PING of Death- Intruder sends a PING that consists of an illegally modified and very large IP datagram, thus overfilling the system buffers and causing the system to reboot or hang.

SYN Attack
■ Attacks the buffer space during a Transmission Control Protocol (TCP)
■ Attacker floods the target system's 'in-process' queue with connection requests causing the system to time-out.

Teardrop Attack
■ Modifying the length of the fragmentation fields in the IP Packet
■ When a machine receives this attack, it is unable to handle the data and can exhibit behavior ranging from a lost Internet connection to the infamous blue screen of death. Becomes confuse and crashes.

Smurf Attack
■ (Source Site) Sends spoofed network request to large network (bounce site) all machines respond to the (target site). IP broadcast addressing.

Fraggle Attack
■ The "smurf" attack's cousin is called "fraggle", which uses UDP echo packets in the same fashion as the ICMP echo packet.

Common Session Hijacking Attacks
■ **IP Spoofing** – IP spoofing is used to convince a system that it is communicating with a known entity that gives an intruder access. IP spoofing involves altering the packet at the TCP level. The attacker sends a packet with an IP source address of a known, trusted source. E-mail spoofing is the forgery of an e-mail header so that the message appears to have originated from someone or somewhere other than the actual source.
■ **TCP Sequence number** – tricks the target in believing that it's connected to a trusted host and then hijacks the session by predicting the target's choice of an initial TCP Sequence number. Then it's used to launch various other attacks on other hosts.

Salami Attack: A series of minor computer crimes that are part of a larger crime.

Rainbow Series
■ Redbook – TNI - Trusted Network Interpretation
■ Time and technological changes lessen the relevancy of the TNI to contemporary networking.
■ Deals with technical issues outside the scope of the Orange Book wrt to networks
■ Redbook interprets the Orange Book
■ Orange Book – Trusted Computer Security Evaluation Criteria

TNI Evaluation Classes
D – Minimal protection
C – Discretionary protection
C1 – Discretionary Security Protection
C2 – Controlled Access protection
B – Mandatory
B1 – Labeled Security
B2 – Structured
B3- Security Domains

Technology Concepts
Protocols: is a standard set of rules that determines how computers communicate with each other across networks despite their differences (PC, UNIC, Mac..)
Layered architecture: shows how communication should take place
■ Clarify the general functions of a communication process
■ To break down complex networking processes into more manageable sublayers
■ Using industry-standard interfaces enables interoperability
■ To change the features of one layer without changing all of the code in every layer
■ Easier troubleshooting

OSI – Open Systems Interconnect Model

Layer	Name	Security / Technology / Protocols	Description
Layer 7	**Application**	**Security**: Confidentiality, authentication, data integrity, non-repudiation **Technology**: gateways **Protocols**: FTP, SMB, TELNET, TFTP, SMTP, HTTP, NNTP, CDP, GOPHER, SNMP, NDS, AFP, SAP, NCP, SET	■ Responsible for all application-to-application communications. User information maintained at this layer is ***user data***.
Layer 6	**Presentation**	**Security**: confidentiality, authentication, encryption **Technology**: gateway **Protocols**: ASCII, EBCDIC, POSTSCRIPT, JPEG, MPEG, GIF	■ Responsible for the formatting of the data so that it is suitable for presentation. Responsible for character conversion (ASCII/EBCDIC), Encryption/Decryption, Compression, and Virtual Terminal Emulation. User information maintained at this layer is called ***messages***.
Layer 5	**Session**	**Security**: None **Technology**: gateways **Protocols**: Remote Procedure Calls (RPC) and SQL, RADIUS, DNS, ASP	■ Responsible for the setup of the links, maintaining of the link, and the link tear-down between applications.
Layer 4	**Transport**	**Security**: Confidentiality, authentication, integrity **Technology**: gateways **Protocols**: TCP, UDP, SSL, SSH-2, SPX, NetBios, ATP	■ Responsible for the guaranteed delivery of user information. It is also responsible for error detection, correction, and flow control. User information at this layer is called ***datagrams***.
Layer 3	**Network**	**Security**: confidentiality, authentication, data integrity **Technology**: virtual circuits (ATM), routers **Protocols**: IP, IPX, ICMP, OSPF, IGRP, EIGRP, RIP, BOOTP, DHCP, ISIS, ZIP, DDP, X.25	■ Responsible for the routing of user data from one node to another through the network including the path selection. Logical addresses are used at this layer. User information maintained at this layer is called ***packets***.
Layer 2	**Data Link**	**Security**: confidentiality, **Technology**: bridges, switch **Protocols**: L2F, PPTP, L2TP, PPP, SLIP, ARP, RARP, SLARP, IARP, SNAP, BAP, CHAP, LCP, LZS, MLP, Frame Relay, Annex A, Annex D, HDLC, BPDU, LAPD, ISL, MAC, Ethernet, Token Ring, FDDI	■ Responsible for the physical addressing of the network via MAC addresses. Ther are two sublevels to the Data-Link layer. MAC and LLC. The Data-Link layer has error detection, frame ordering, and flow control. User information maintained at this layer is called ***frames***.
Layer 1	**Physical**	**Security**: confidentiality **Technology**: ISDN, Hubs, Repeaters, Cables **Protocols**: 10BaseT, 100BaseT, 1000BaseT, 10Base2, 10Base5, OC-3, OC-12, DS1, DS3, E1, E3, ATM, BRI, PRI, X.23	■ Responsible for the physical transmission of the binary digits through the physical medium. This layer includes things such as the physical cables, interfaces, and data rate specifications. User information maintained at this layer is called ***bits*** (the 1s and 0s).

Data encapsulation is the process in which information from one packet is wrapped around or attached to the data of another packet. In OSI model each layer encapsulates the layer immediately above it.

OSI Layers
- Process down the stack and up the stack
- Each layer communicates with corresponding layer through the stack.

OSI Security - 6 Security Services. A security service is a collection of security mechanisms, files, and procedures that help protect the network.
- Authentication
- Access control
- Data confidentiality
- Data integrity
- Non-repudiation
- Logging and monitoring

OSI Security - 8 Security Mechanisms. A security mechanism is a control that is implemented in order to provide the 6 basic security services.
- Encipherment
- Digital signature
- Access Control
- Data Integrity
- Authentication
- Traffic Padding
- Routing Control
- Notarization

TCP/IP – Suite of Protocols

OSI	TCP/IP	Protocols	Description
Application	Application Layer		Consists of the applications and processes that use the network.
Presentation			
Session			
Transport	Host to Host	TCP and UDP	Provides end-to-end data delivery service to the Application Layer.
Network	Internet Layer	IP, ARP, RARP, ICMP	Defines the IP datagram and handles the routing of data across networks.
Data link	Network Access		Consists of routines for accessing physical networks and the electrical connection.
Physical			

Host-to-Host Transport Layer Protocols:
TCP – Transmission Control Protocol
- Connection Oriented
- Sequenced Packets
- Acknowledgment is sent back for received packets
- If no acknowledgement then packet is resent
- Packets are re-sequenced
- Manageable data flow is maintained

NOTE: TCP and UDP use port numbers greater than 1023

UDP
- Best effort
- Doesn't care about sequence order
- Connectionless

- Less overhead and faster than TCP

Internet Layer Protocols
IP – Internet Protocol
- All hosts on a network have an IP address
- Each data packet is assigned the IP address of the sender and receiver
- It provides an 'unreliable datagram service'. Provides:
  - No guarantees that the packet will be delivered
  - No guarantee that the packet will be delivered only once
  - No guarantee that it will be delivered in the order which it was sent

ARP – Address Resolution Protocol
- Use the IP Address to get the MAC Address
- MAC address is 48 bit
- IP address is 32 bit
- Only broadcast to network first time, otherwise stores IP and MAC info in table

RARP – Reverse Address Resolution Protocol
- Use the MAC Address to get the IP Address
- RARP Server tells diskless machines IP Address

ICMP – Internet Control Message Protocol
- Management Protocol and messaging service provider for IP.
- Sends messages between network devices regarding the health of the network.
- Ping is ICMP packet
- Ping checks if a host is up and operational

TCP/IP Does not define Physical Standards it uses existing ones

Other TCP/IP Protocols
- **Telnet** – Terminal Emulation (No File Transfer)
- **FTP** – File Transfer Protocol – (Can not execute files)
- **TFTP** – Trivial FTP – no directory browsing capabilities, no authentication (it is unsecure), can only send and receive files.
  - Some sites choose not to implement TFTP due to the inherent security risks.
  - TFTP is an UDP-based file transfer program that provides no security.
- **NFS** – Network File Sharing
- **SMTP** – Delivers emails
- **LDP** – Line Printer Daemon – with LPR enables print spooling
- **X-Windows** – for writing graphical interface application
- **SNMP** – Simple Network Management Protocol
  - Provides for the collection of network information by polling the devices on the network from a management station.
  - Sends SNMP traps (notification) to MIBS Management Information Bases
- **Bootstrap (BootP) protocol** – Diskless boot up. BootP server hears the request and looks up the client's MAC address in its BootP file. It's an internet layer protocol.

Security Enhanced Protocols (Two types)
Security enhancements to telnet such as remote terminal access and secure telnet
Security enhancements to Remote Procedure Call such as Secure RPC Authentication

Following Security Protocols:
At the Application Layer (OSI Model)
SET – Secure Electronic Transaction
- Originated by Visa and MasterCard
- Being overtaken by SSL

SHTTP - Secure HTTP
- Early standard for encrypting HTTP documents
- Also being overtaken by SSL

At the Transport Layer (OSI Model)
SSH-2
- SSH has RSA Certificates
- Supports authentication, compression, confidentiality, and integrity
- DES Encryption
- Because Secure Shell (SSH-2) supports authentication, compression, confidentiality, and integrity, SSH is used frequently for Encrypted File Transfer

SSL – Secure Socket Layer
- Contains SSL record protocol and SSL Handshake Protocol
- Uses symmetric encryption and public key for authentication
- MAC – Message Authentication Code for Integrity

SKIP – Simple Key Management for Internet Protocol
Similar to SSL – no prior communication required

Firewalls
Packet Filtering Firewall - First Generation
- Screening Router
- Operates at Network and Transport level
- Examines Source and Destination IP Address
- Can deny based on ACLs
- Can specify Port

Application Level Firewall - Second Generation
- Proxy Server
- Copies each packet from one network to the other
- Masks the origin of the data
- Operates at layer 7 (Application Layer)
- Reduces Network performance since it has do analyze each packet and decide what to do with it.
- Also Called Application Layer Gateway

Stateful Inspection Firewalls – Third Generation
- Packets Analyzed at all OSI layers
- Queued at the network level
- Faster than Application level Gateway

Dynamic Packet Filtering Firewalls – Fourth Generation
- Allows modification of security rules
- Mostly used for UDP
- Remembers all of the UDP packets that have crossed the network's perimeter, and it decides whether to enable packets to pass through the firewall.

Kernel Proxy – Fifth Generation
- Runs in NT Kernel
- Uses dynamic and custom TCP/IP-based stacks to inspect the network packets and to enforce security policies.

Firewall Architectures:

Packet Filtering Routers:
- Sits between trusted and untrusted networks
- Uses ACLs
- ACLs can be manually intensive to maintain
- Lacks strong user authentication
- ACLs can degrade performance
- Minimal Auditing

Screened Host Firewall:
- Employs packet filtering and Bastion Host
- Provides network layer (packet filtering) and application layer (proxy) services
- Penetration requires getting by external router (packet filtering) and Bastion Host (proxy).

Dual Homed Host Firewall
- Contains two NICs
- One connected to the local "trusted" network
- One connected to the external "untrusted" network
- Blocks or filters traffic between the two.
- IP forwarding is disabled

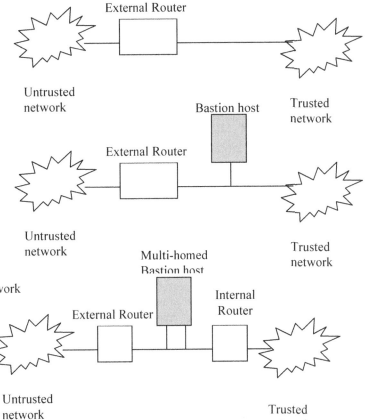

Screened Subnet Firewall

- One of the most secure
- Two packet filtering routers and a Bastion Host
- Provides network layer (packet filtering) and application layer (proxy) services
- Provides DMZ
- Complex configuration

DMZ

Multi-homed
Bastion host

External Router

Internal
Router

Untrusted
network

Trusted
network

SOCKS Server

- Circuit level proxy server
- Requires SOCKS client on all machines
- Used to manage outbound Internet access
- IT Overhead intensive

NAT – Network Address Translation

3 Private IP Address Ranges – Global Nonroutable Addresses

10.0.0.0 to 10.255.255.255
172.16.0.0 to 172.31.255.255
192.168.0.0 to 192.168.255.255

- Class A addresses are for large networks with many devices. 1-127
- Class B addresses are for medium-sized networks. 128-191
- Class C addresses are for small networks (fewer than 256 devices). 192-223
- Class D addresses are multicast addresses.

Virtual Private Networks:

- Secure connection between two nodes using secret encapsulation method.
- Secure Encrypted Tunnel – encapsulated tunnel (encryption may or may not be used)
- Tunnel can be created by the following three methods:
    - Installing software or agents on client or network gateway.
    - Implementing user or node authentication systems.
    - Implementing key and certificate exchange systems.

VPN Protocol Standards:

PPTP – Point-to-Point Tunneling Protocol

- Works at the Data Link Layer
- Single point to point connection from client to server
- Common with asynchronous connections with NT and Win 95

L2TP - Layer 2 Tunneling Protocol

- Combination of PPTP and earlier Layer 2 Forwarding Protocol (L2F)
- Multiple protocols can be encapsulated within the L2TP
- Single point to point connection from client to server
- Common with Dial up VPNs

IPSec

- Operates at the network layer
- Allows multiple and simultaneous tunnels
- Encrypt and authenticate IP data
- Focuses more on Network to Network Connectivity

VPN Devices

- Hardware and Software devices that utilize VPN Standards
- Two types: IPSec Compatible and Non-IPSec Compatible

IPSec Compatible
- Installed on a networks perimeter and encrypt traffic between the two
- Because IPSec only work with IP
- Operate at Network Layer
- **Two Modes**:
  - **Tunnel Mode** – entire packet is encrypted and encases in IPSec packet
  - **Transport Mode** – Only datagram is encrypted leaving IP address visible.
- **Datagram**: A self-contained, independent entity of data carrying sufficient information to be routed from the source to the destination.

Non-IPSec Compatible
- Common non-IPSec compatible include SOCKS, PPTP and SSH
- SOCKS is not traditional VPN protocol but is robust and operates at Application Layer.
- PTP implemented in Win95 and NT
  - Multiprotocol and uses PAP and CHAP user authentication.
  - Compresses Data
  - End-to-End encryption
- Secure Shell SSH-2
  - Not strictly VPN but can be used as one with Terminal Session

Firewall Based VPNs
- Frequently available with Third Generation (Stateful Inspection) Firewalls
- Operate at the Application layer
- Performance degradation is often a problem

Data Networking Basics

Data Network Types:
- Local Area Network (LAN)
- Wide Area Network (WAN)
- Internet, Intranet, and Extranet

Local Area Networks – LAN
- Discrete network for limited geographical area like a building or a single floor
- Two most popular LANs are:
  - **CAN - Campus Area Network** – connects multiple buildings with each other over switched backbone
  - **MAN – Metropolitan Area Network** – LAN over a city wide metropolitan area.
- Both CAN and MAN can have a connection to WAN

Wide Area Networks - WAN
- Network of sub networks that interconnect LANs over large geographic areas.
- WAN is basically everything outside of LAN

Internet
- The Internet is a WAN originally funded by the DOD
- Uses TCP/IP

Intranet
- Internet like logical network that uses a companies internal physical network structure
- More security and control than Internet
- Uses Internet tools like browsers.

Extranet
- Extranet can be accessed by users outside of the company, (i.e. vendors and partners) but not the general public.

■ Includes some type of authentication or encryption

Asynchronous vs. Synchronous Communications
■ Asynchronous is basis of modems and dial up remote access. Must operate at same speed.
  ■ Start and stop bits mark the beginning and the end of each transfer.
■ Synchronous is very high speed, governed by electronic clock timing signals.

Common Data Network Services:

Files Services – Share data files and subdirectories on file server

Mail Services – send and receive mail internally and externally

Print Services – Print documents to shared printers

Client/ Server Services – Allocate computing resources among workstations

Domain Name Service – Matches Internet Uniform Resource Locator (URL) with the actual IP address of the server providing the URL. Maps host names to IP Addresses. The Domain Name System (DNS) is a global network of servers that provide this service.

Data Networking Technologies:

LAN Cabling Types:

Twisted Pair Cable
■ Relatively slow speed
■ Two insulated wires can be shielded (STP) or unshielded (UTP)
■ UTP is a four-pair medium comes in several categories
■ UTP can be easily tapped by eavesdroppers than the other cable types.
■ Category based on how tightly wound the wires are, tighter the wind the higher the rating and resistance to interference.
■ Cat 1 UTP– was used for telephone lines not good for data.
■ Cat 2 UTP – up to 4 MBps
■ Cat 3 UTP – Used for 10BaseT networks up to 10 MBps
■ Cat 4 UTP – Used in Token Ring Networks up to 16 MBps
■ Cat 5 UTP - Current UTP standard for new installations up to 100 MBps
■ Cat 6 UTP – up to 155 MBps
■ Cat 7 UTP – up to 1 GBps

Coaxial Cable
■ Hollow outer conductor surrounds inner wire conductor. Currently two types in LANs
  ■ 50-ohm Cable for digital signaling
  ■ 75-ohm Cable for analog signaling and high speed digital signaling
■ Coax is more expensive but is more resistant to Electromagnetic Interference (EMI).
■ Used rarely except in Broadband communications
■ Comes in two types:
  ■ **Thinnet** – (RG58)
  ■ **Thicknet** – (RG8 or RG11)
■ Two common types of coaxial transmission methods:
  ■ **Baseband** – The cable carries a single channel
  ■ **Broadband** – cable carries several channels such as data, voice, audio, and video

Fiber Optic Cable
■ Conducts modulated light transmission
■ Light waves are faster and travel greater distances

- Difficult to tap
- Resistant to EMI
- Usually connects backbones in larger networks
- Can be used to connect workstations to the network.
- Expensive to install and to terminate.

LAN Transmission Protocols:
- Rules for communication between computers on a LAN
- Formatting of the data frame, the timing and sequencing of packet delivery, and resolution of error states.

Carrier Sense Multiple Access (CSMA)
- Foundation of Ethernet Protocol.
- Workstation continuously monitors the line waiting until it thinks it is free.
- If the workstation doesn't receive an acknowledgement from the destination to which it sent the packet, it assumes a collision has occurred and it resends the packet.
  - Persistent Carrier Sense - Unless receives acknowledgement it will resend.
  - Nonpersistent Carrier Sense – waits random amount of time and resends.

CSMA/CA - Carrier Sense Multiple Access Collision Avoidance – Workstations connected to two coax cables, one to send and one to receive data.

CSMA/CD - Carrier Sense Multiple Access Collision Detection – **Ethernet**
If the host detects another signal while transmitting it will send a jam signal causing all nodes to stop sending data. Nodes wait to resend. Designed to avoid collisions.

Polling – a primary workstation polls another at a predetermined time to determine if it has data to transmit. Primary must give permission to others to transmit.

Token passing
- Token Ring and FDDI and ARCnet
- Cannot transmit without the token
- Each station can hold token for maximum predetermined amount of time

LAN Transmission Methods: refer to the way packets are sent on the network
- Unicast – from single source to single destination
- Multicast - source copied and sent to multiple destinations
- Broadcast - source copied and sent to all nodes on the network

LAN Topologies Five common topologies: defines the manner in which the network devices are organized to facilitate communications.
Bus
- All transmissions travel full length of the cable and received by all other stations.
- Single point of failure in the cable.
- If one of the links between any of the computers is broken, the network is down.
- Primarily Ethernet.
- These networks were originally designed to work with more sporadic traffic.

Ring
- Unidirectional transmission links form closed loop.
- Token Ring and FDDI.
- Similar to the Star topology, however there's a device called a Multistation Access Unit (MAU).
- MAU works the same as a hub, but with Token Ring networks instead of Ethernet networks.
- These networks were originally designed to serve large, bandwidth-consuming applications.

Star
- Nodes connected to a central LAN or a junction box called a hub or a concentrator at the center of the network.
- Ads: reliability
- Ring and Bus often use Star as physical connection.

Tree – branches can have multiple nodes.

Mesh – all nodes connected to every other node.

LAN Media Access Methods (Physical and Data Link Layers): control the use of a network.
Ethernet – 802.3
- Ethernet – uses CSMA/CD – Designed for sporadic traffic
- Ethernet defines a bus topology with three different cabling standards
  - Thinnet – 10Base2 – coax with segments up to 185 meters.
  - Thicknet – 10BaseS – coax with segments up to 500 meters.
  - UTP – Unshielded Twisted Pair – all devices connected to a hub or switch 10BaseT 10 Mbps, 100BaseT 100 Mbps and 1000BaseT 1 GBps

ARCnet – 802.5
- Early LAN technologies
- Uses token passing in a Star topology on coax cable.

Token Ring
- Second to Ethernet
- All end stations connected to a Multistation Access Unit (MSAU)
- One station is designated as the Active Monitor
- If a transmitting station fails, the Active monitor will remove the token and generate a new one.

Fiber Distributed Data Interface – FDDI
- Dual token ring LAN at 100 MBps on Fiber
- Dual counter rotating rings only one active at a time
- Operates over long distances with minimal interference
- Predictable delays, deterministic
- Permits several tokens to be present at a time
- Expensive and requires expertise
- Copper Distributed Data Interface (CDDI) – can be used with UTP cable but subject to interference and length issues associated with Copper.

LAN Devices
Repeaters – amplify signal, no added intelligence, no filtering – **Physical Layer (1)**
Hubs – used to connect multiple LAN devices, no added intelligence – **Physical Layer (1)**
Bridges – Amplify signal, add some intelligence. A bridge forwards the data to all other network segments if the Media Access Control (MAC) or hardware address of the destination computer is not on the local network segment. Automatically forwards all broadcast traffic. Does not use IP address because IP is contained in the Network Layer (3) – **Data Link Layer (2)**
Switches – Will only send data to the port where the destination MAC address is, not to all ports. Primarily operate at the **Data Link Layer (2),** although extremely fast layer 3 devices combining switching and routing are being used.
Routers – router opens packet and looks at either the MAC or IP address only forwards to the network that it is destined. Operates at **Network Layer (3)**
Gateways – primarily software, can be multi-protocol, can examine entire packet.
Asynchronous Transfer Mode (ATM) Switches – Used in WANs and CANs. Use cell relay technology.
LAN Extenders – remote access multi layer switch connected to host router, filters based on MAC address or Network Layer protocol, not capable of firewalling.

WAN Technologies
Rules for communicating between computers on a WAN
Communications between large disparate networks.

Private Circuit Technologies
Evolved before packet switching networks. Dedicated analog or digital point-to-point connection. Serial Line Internet Protocol (SLIP), Point-to Point protocol (PPP), ISDN, xDSL.

- Dedicated Line – indefinitely and continuously reserve for transmissions.
- Leased Line – Type of dedicated line leased from carrier.

Types and Speeds of Leased Lines:
- **Digital Signal Level 0** – DS-0 – single channel at 64KBps on a T1
- **Digital Signal Level 1** – DS-1 – 1.544 MBps in US on a T1 and 2.108 MBps in Europe on a E1
- **Digital Signal Level 3** – DS-3 – 44.736 MBps on a T3

- **T1** – Transmits DS-1 data at 1.544 MBps on telephone switching network
- **T3** – Transmits DS-3 data at 44.736 MBps on telephone switching network

- **E1** – predominately used in Europe carries data at 2.108 MBps
- **E3** - predominately used in Europe carries data at 34.368 MBps

SLIP - Serial Line Internet Protocol – developed in 1984 to support TCP/IP over low speed serial interfaces. Using Windows NT RAS, NT computers can use TCP/IP and SLIP to communicate to remote hosts.

PPP - Point-to Point protocol – over dial up and dedicated links, includes login, password, and error correction. Operates at the Data Link Layer (2) and uses CHAP and PAP.

ISDN - Integrated Services Digital Network - integration of digital telephony and data transport. Digitization of the telephone network, allowing voice, data, etc. Overtaken by DSL.

xDSL - Digital Subscriber Line – uses existing twisted pair telephone lines.
- ADSL – Asymmetric Digital Subscriber Line more bandwidth downstream from 1.5 to 9 MBps with upstream 16 to 640 KBps. ADSL works at 18,000 feet lengths, theoretical and 14,400 practical over single copper twisted pair.
- SDSL - Single-line (Symmetric) Digital Subscriber Line provides from 144 KBps up to 1.544 MBps both down and up, depending on distance, over single copper twisted pair, works at 10,000 feet lengths.
- HDSL – High-Rate Digital Subscriber Line - 1.544 MBps both down and up over two copper twisted pair. Provides T1 speeds. Can do 2.048 MBps on three copper twisted pair.
- VDSL – Very-high Rate Digital Subscriber Line – 13-52 MBps down and 1.5 MB to 2.3 MBps upstream over single copper twisted pair operating range 1,000 – 4,500 feet

Circuit Switched vs. Packet Switched

Circuit Switched
- Defined as a switching system in which a physical circuit path must exist for the duration of the transmission
- Physical permanent connections from one point to another
- Older technology than Packet Switching
- Phone companies use this a lot

Packet Switched
- Create virtual circuits used as needed and reduce cost.
- Defined as a switching system where nodes share bandwidth by sending small packets.
- Each packet sent to the next destination by the router.
- Packets reassembled based on original sequence

Message switching – Message sent from node to node and stored at each node until forwarding path is available

Packet Switching Technologies – X.25, Link Access Procedure Balance (LABP), Frame Relay, Switched Multimegabit Data Service (SMDS), Asynchronous Transfer Mode (ATM), Voice over IP (VoIP)

X.25
- First packet switching network
- Supports Switched Virtual Circuits (SVCs) and Permanent Virtual Circuits (PVCs)
- Designed to operate effectively regardless of the type of systems connected to
- Currently much more predominant overseas than in the US

Link Access Procedure Balance (LAPB)
- Designed for use with X.25
- Defines frame types
- Can retransmit, exchange and detect out of sequence frames or missing frames.

Frame Relay
- High performance WAN protocol
- Operates at Physical and Data Link Layers (1 and 2)
- Originally designed for ISDN
- Replaces X.25 and LAPB
- Simple and fast, no error correcting
- Supports Switched Virtual Circuits (SVCs) and Permanent Virtual Circuits (PVCs)
- Not available everywhere

Switched Multimegabit Data Service (SMDS)
- High Speed over public switched networks
- Connectionless bandwidth on demand

Asynchronous Transfer Mode (ATM)
- High bandwidth, low delay
- Uses switching and multiplexing
- Uses 53 byte fixed size cells instead of frames
- Can allocate bandwidth on demand
- Taking place of FDDI in Campus Backbone

Voice Over IP
- Combines media types (voice, video, data, audio) into one IP packet
- Provides benefits in cost, performance and interoperability
- Very new but far reaching potential

Other Important WAN Protocols

Synchronous Data Link Control (SDLC)
- Uses polling access method for mainframes
- Based on dedicated leased line
- Evolved into HDLC and LAPB
- Operates at **Data Link Layer (2)**

High-Level Data Link Control (HDLC)
- Derived from SDLC
- Specifies data encapsulation method on synchronous serial links
- Operates at **Data Link Layer (2)**

High Speed Serial Interface
- Defines the electrical and physical interfaces to be used by DTE/DCE
- Operates and the **Physical Layer (1)**

WAN Devices

Routers – router opens packet and looks at either the MAC or IP address only forwards to the network that it is destined.   Operates at Network Layer (3)

Multiplexors - MUX enables more than one signal to be sent out over one physical circuit

WAN Switches – multi-port network devices operate at the Data Link Layer (2). Typically switch Frame Relay, X.25 and SMDS

Access Servers – provides dial in and dial out access connections to a network. Typically asynchronous.

Modems – interprets digital and analog signals, transmits over voice grade telephone lines.

Channel Service Unit (CSU)/Data Service Unit (DSU) – used to terminate the physical interface on a DTE device such as a terminal.

Remote Access Technologies
Provide remote user (employee, vendor, partner) access into the network while maintaining C.I.A. (Confidentiality, Integrity, Availability)

Benefits of Remote Access:
- Reducing costs by replacing dedicated network lines
- Providing employees flexible work styles, Telecommuting
- Building efficient ties with vendors, partners, suppliers and employees.

Remote Access Types – Many common with WAN protocols.

Asynchronous Dial up Access
- How most people access Internet
- Use existing public switched phone network to access ISP

ISDN - Integrated Services Digital Network
- Carries voice, data over telephone networks
- Two Interface Types
- **BRI** – Basic Rate Interface composed of two B channels and one D Channel
- **PRI** – Primary Rate Interface composed of a single 64 KBps D channel plus 23(T1) or 30 (E1) channels

xDSL - Digital Subscriber Line
- Uses existing twisted pair telephone lines.

Cable Modems
- High speed access from the cable company
- Users share the Coax connection

- Throughput varies depending on number of users
- Considered insecure because local segment is not filtered or firewalled (Says Who?)

Wireless Technology
- Fastest Growing area of connectivity
- Encryption is being developed
- 802.11a – 5 Ghz wireless - very soon
- 802.11b – 2.4 Ghz currently most popular up to 11 MBps
- 802.11g – 2.4 Ghz but faster than 802.11b
- WEP – Wired Equivalency Protocol – up to 128-bit WEP
- WAP - Wireless Access Point
- SSID – Service Set Identifier – Network Name
- Use encryption, VPN, treat as external connection, directional antenna

Secure Remote Access Methods:
Restricted Address
- Filtering by source IP address
- Node authentication not user authentication

Caller ID
- Caller ID checks incoming number against approved list
- Very commonly used, hard to defeat
- Hard to administer for traveling users

Call Back
- Caller supplies password or identifier and hangs up
- System dials back number listed for the user
- Hard to administer for traveling users

Remote Identification and Authentication
- Verify who is remotely communication.
- Identification - Who
- Authentication – Verify and Trust

Remote Node Security Protocols:
Password Authentication Protocol (PAP)
- Remote security protocol. Provides Identification and Authentication.
- Uses static replayable password for authentication (now considered weak)
- Does not encrypt the User ID or Password

Challenge Handshake Protocol (CHAP)
- Next evolution of PAP uses stronger authentication
- Nonreplayable Challenge/Response
- Verifies Identity of the node
- Often used to enable network-to-network communication
- Commonly used by remote access servers and xDSL, ISDN, and cable modems

Remote Access Authentication Systems:
- TACACS – Terminal Access Controller Access Control System **(TCP)**
- TACACS+ – includes the use of two factor authentication
- RADIUS – Remote Access Dial-In User Service **(UDP)**

TACACS – Terminal Access Controller Access Control System
- Provides remote authentication and related services
- User password administered in a central database rather than in individual routers
- TACACS enabled network device prompts for user name and **static password**

- TACACS enabled network device queries TACACA server to verify password
- Does not support prompting for password change or use of dynamic tokens

TACACS+ Terminal Access Controller Access Control System Plus
- Proprietary CISCO enhancement
- Two factor Authentication
- User can change password
- Ability to use secure tokens
- Better Audit Trails

RADIUS – Remote Access Dial-In User Service
- Offers similar benefits to TACACS+
- Often used as a stepping stone to TACACS+
- Radius Server contains **dynamic password** and network service access information (Network ACLS)
- Radius is a fully open protocol, can be customized for almost any security system
- Can be used with Kerberos and provides CHAP remote node authentication
- Except does not work with:
  - Apple Talk Remote Access Resolution Protocol
  - NetBios Frame Protocol Control Protocol
  - Netware Asynchronous Services Interface
  - X.25 PAD Connection

Does not provide two-way authentication and is not used for router-to-router authentication.

Domain 4 – Cryptography

Purpose of Cryptography is to protect information from being read and understood by anyone except the intended recipient.

In practice encryption can be a function of time, the effort and time required for an unauthorized person is so large it is impractical. By the time it is decrypted it is of little value.

Block Cipher – Breaks the plaintext into blocks and encrypts each with the same algorithm

Cipher – Cryptographic transformation operates on the characters or bites

Ciphertext or Cryptogram – unintelligible message

Clustering – plaintext message generates identical ciphertext using the same algorithm but different keys

Codes – A cryptographic transformation that operates at the word or phrase level

Cryptanalysis – act of obtaining plaintext or key from ciphertext

Cryptographic Algorithm – Step-by-step procedure used to encipher plaintext and decipher ciphertext

Cryptography – Art and Science of hiding the meaning of communication

Cryptology – encompasses cryptography and cryptanalysis

Cryptosystem – set of transformations from message space to ciphertext space

Decipher - to undo cipherment process

Encipher – to make a message unintelligible to all except recipient

End-to-end encryption – Encrypted information that is sent from sender to receiver

Exclusive Or
- Boolean Operation
- Indicated by XOR
- Indicated by symbol $\otimes$
- Easily implemented in hardware
- 0+0=0, 0+1=1, 1+1=0, 1+1=0

Input A	Input B	Output T
0	0	0
0	1	1
1	0	1
1	1	0

- XOR operated on the bit level
- XOR the plain text (byte level) with the keystream source
- Can be reversed by simple XOR of output plus keystream.
    - A XOR B = T
    - T XOR B = A

Key – cryptovariable
- Information or sequence that controls enciphering and deciphering of message

Link Encryption
- Each entity has key in common with two neighboring nodes.
- Node 1 –Encrypts with key A
- Node 2 – Decrypts with key A and encrypts with key B
- Node 3 – Decrypts with Key B and encrypts with Key C

One time pad
- Encryption with key K with components k1, k2,…kn, the encipherment uses each component of k to encrypt message M with components m1, m2,…mn.
- The Key is the same length as the Message
- Key only used once and never again
- Key must be completely random
- Not very practical
- Used
- Invented 1917 by the US Army Signal Corps and AT&T

Plaintext – a message in clear text

Steganogrophy
- Secret communication of a message where communication is hidden
- Example – last bit of each pixel in an image file contains bit of a message.

Work Function (Factor)
- Difficulty in recovering plain text from ciphertext as a factor of time and cost
- Systems security is directly proportional to the work function
- Work function should be commensurate with the value of the data

History of Cryptography
Traced back to the Egyptians in 3000B.C.

Scytale
- used by Spartans in 400B.C. – wrap message around wooden dowel
- diameter and length are the keys to the cipher.

Caesar cipher
- Monoalphabetic substitution – only used one alphabet
- Specifically - Involved shifting the alphabet three letters
- Known as C3 (Caesar shift 3 places)

Cipher Disks
- Two concentric disks with letters on the edge
- Can be used to match up letters

Arabs invented cryptanalysis
- Arab philosopher al-Kindi wrote Manuscript on Deciphering Cryptographic Messages

Thomas Jefferson - disks
- 1790 developed device with 26 disks that could be rotated individually
- Message would assembled by lining up the disks to the alignment bar
- Then the bar was rotated a given angle and the resulting letters were the cipher text
- The angle of rotation of the alignment bar was the key

Disks used extensively during the civil war

UNIX – ROT13 shift the alphabet 13 places

Hagelin Machine
- Developed in 1920 by Boris Hagelin – Stockholm Sweden
- Known as the M-209 in the US

1920'a Herbert O. Yardley was in charge of U.S. MI-8 (a.k.a. the Black Chamber)
- Cracked codes of a number of Nations
- Gave U.S edge in Japanese negotiations in 1921-1922
- U.S. State Department shut down MI-8
- Upset, Yardley published book The American Black Chamber 1931
- Japanese got new codes
- Yardley is father of American Cryptology

Japanese Purple Machine
After Yardley William Friedman resumed cryptanalysis for U.S. Army
Broke the new Japanese cipher.
U.S. Navy broke the Purple Machine naval codes during World War II

German Enigma Machine
- Polyalphabetic substitution cipher - using mechanical rotors
- Developed in 1919 by Dutchman Arthur Scherbius obtained US Patent for Berlin firm
- Polish cryptanalyst broke the three-ring system with card file of all 6 x 17,576 possible rotor positions
- 1938 German went to six rings
- In 1938 Poles and French developed the "Bombe" there own Enigma machine
- British took over in 1940 and by 1943 British and US had high speed "bombe"
- Disks have 26 contacts on each side, to communicate with each neighboring disk one of them makes contact with the other disk
- Also rotates the disks after encryption of each letter
- Rotates next highest rotor like a "gas pump" – polyalphabetic
- Other rotor machines – German Enigma, Japanese Red, Japanese Purple and American SIGABA "Big Machine"

Cryptographic Technologies
Symmetric Key - (Private Key or Secret Key)
Asymmetric Key – (Public Key)

Public Key cannot derive the private Key
Private Key Cryptography is 1,000 times faster than public key cryptography

Vigenere Polyalphabetic Cipher
- Caesar is a subset of the Vigenere Polyalphabetic Cipher
- Vigenere used 26 alphabets
- Each letter of the message corresponds to a different alphabet
- Subject to guessing the period, when the alphabet changes

Modulo returns the remainder over the modulo value
$C=(M+b) \bmod N$
Where
C = Cipher Text
M= Message
B = fixed integer
N = size of alphabet

Transposition – Permutation
- Columnar Transposition – write the message vertically and read horizontally
- Can be attacked through frequency analysis

Vernam Cipher - One time pad, random set of non-repeating characters
Book or Running Key Cipher
- Using text from a book as the key and performing modulo26 addition on it.
- Would use specific line and page number

Codes - Deal with words and phrases and represent them with other numbers or letter
Concealment cipher: Every X number of words within a text, is a part of the real message.

Steganogrophy
- Hiding the existence of the message.
- A digital watermark would be used to detect copying of digital images

Secret Key Cryptography – Symmetric Key
- Sender and receiver both know the key
- Encrypt and decrypt with the same key
- Secret key should be changed frequently
- Requires secure distribution of keys – by alternate channel
- Ideally only used once
- Secret Key Cryptosystem does have both public and private information
  - **Public**
  - Algorithm for enciphering plaintext
  - Possibly some plaintext and cipher text
  - Possibly encipherment of chosen plaintext
  - **Private**
  - The KEY
  - One cryptographic transformation out of many possible transformations
- Large keys like >128 bit are very hard to break
- Very fast
- Sender requires different key for each receiver
- Time stamps can be associated to the key so valid only during time window (counters replay)
- No Authentication or repudiation
- Best known is DES developed by IBM in 1970's for commercial use

DES – Data Encryption Standard
- Derived in 1972 as derivation of Lucifer algorithm developed by Horst Fiestel at IBM
- Patented in 1974 - Block Cipher Cryptographic System
- Commercial and non-classified systems
- DES describes the Data Encryption Algorithm DEA
- Federal Information Processing Standard FIPS adopted DES in 1977
- Re-certified in 1993 by National Institute of Standards and Technology but will be replaced by AES Advanced Encryption Standard by Rijndael.
- DES uses 64 bit block size and 56 bit key, begins with 64 bit key and strips 8 parity bits
- DEA is 16 round cryptosystem designed for implementation in hardware
- 56 bit key = 2^{56} or 70 quadrillion possible keys
- Distributed systems can break it. U.S. Government no longer uses it
- Triple DES – three encryptions using DEA are now being used until AES is adopted

- DES uses **confusion** and **diffusion** as suggested by Claude Shannon
  - **Confusion** conceals statistical connection
    - Accomplished through s-boxes
  - **Diffusion** spread the influence of plaintext character over many ciphertext characters
    - Accomplished through p-boxes

DES Operates in four modes
- Electronic Code Book (ECB)
- Cipher Block Chaining (CBC)
- Cipher Feedback (CFB)
- Output Feedback (OFB)

Electronic Code Book
- Native encryption mode
- Provides the recipe of substitutions and permutations that will be performed on the block of plaintext.
- Data within a file does not have to be encrypted in a certain order.
- Used for small amounts of data, like challenge-response, key management tasks.
- Also used to encrypt PINs in ATM machines.

Cipher Block Chaining
- Each block of text, the key, and the value based on the previous block is processed in the algorithm and applied to the next block of text.

Cipher Feedback
- The previously generated ciphertext from the last encrypted block of data is inputted into the algorithm to generate random values.
- These random values are processed with the current block of plaintext to create ciphertext.
- This mode is used when encrypting individual characters is required.

Output Feedback
- Functioning like a stream cipher by generating a stream of random binary bits to be combined with the plaintext to create ciphertext.
- The ciphertext is fed back to the algorithm to form a portion of the next input to encrypt the next stream of bits.

DES has been broken with Internet network of PC's

DES is considered vulnerable by brute force search of the key – replaced by triple DES and AES

Triple DES
- Double encryption is subject to meet in the middle attack
- Encrypt on one end decrypt on the other and compare the values
- So Triple DES is used
- Can be done several different ways:
  - DES – EDE2 (encrypt key 1, decrypt key 2, encrypt key 1)
  - DES – EE2 (encrypt key 1, encrypt key 2, encrypt key 1)
  - DES –EE3 (encrypt key 1, encrypt key 2, encrypt key 3) - most secure

- Advanced Encryption Standard
- Block Cipher that will replace DES
- Anticipated that Triple DES will remain approved for Government Use
- AES announced by NIST in January 1997 to find replacement for DES

5 Finalists
- MARS
- RC6
- Rijndael
- Serpent
- Blowfish

October 2, 2000 NIST Selected Rijndael
2 Belgian Cryptographers Dr. Daeman and Dr. Rijmen
Will be used by government for sensitive but unclassified documents

Rijndael Block Cipher
- Resistance to all known attacks
- Design Simplicity
- Code compactness and speed on wide variety of platforms
- Iterative block cipher with variable block length and key lengths that can be independently chosen as 128, 192 or 256 bits.
- 3.4×10^{38} possible 128 bit key combinations
- 6.2×10^{57} possible 192 bit key combinations
- 1.1×10^{77} possible 256 bit key combinations
- Intermediate cipher result is called "state" that transformations operate on
- Does not use Feistel transposition structure from DES
- Uses round transformation of 3 layers
    - Non-linear layer
    - Linear mixing layer
    - Key addition layer
- Suitable for High Speed Chips and compact co-processor on smart cards

Twofish
- 128 bit blocks in 16 rounds, up to 256 bit keys
- Developed by Counterpane based on Blowfish (also by Counterpane) - Bruce Schnier
- Employs whitening before first round and after second round
- Need to break whitening keys in addition to Twofish key
- Transposition

IDEA Cipher - International Data Encryption Algorithm
- 64 bit block, 8 rounds, and 128 bit keys
- Used in PGP
- Much more difficult than DES

RC5 – Family of algorithms
- Developed by Ronald Rivest in 1994
- 32, 64 or 128 bit blocks, up to 0 to 255 rounds, 0 to 2048 bit keys
- RSA patented in 1997

Public Key Cryptography
- Employee private and public key
- Public made available to anyone wanting to encrypt a message
- Private key is used to decrypt
- Public Key cannot decrypt the message it encrypted
- Ideally private key cannot be derived from the public key
- The other can decrypt a message encrypted by one of the keys
- Private key is kept private

- Possible through the application of one-way functions. Easy to compute in one direction but difficult to compute the other way
- In order to be useful should have a trap door, a secret mechanism that enables you to accomplish the reverse function in a one way function
- 1,000 to 10,000 times slower than secret key encryption
- Hybrids use public key to encrypt the symmetric key
- Important algorithms Diffie-Helllman RSA, El Gamal, Knapsack, Elliptic Curve

RSA
- Rivest, Shamir and Addleman
- Based on difficulty of factoring a number which is the product of two large prime numbers, may be 200 digits each.
- Can be used for Encryption, key exchange, and digital signatures

Diffie-Hellman
- Exchange secret keys over insecure medium without exposing keys
- Without additional session key
- Primarily key exchange

El Gamal
- Extended Diffie-Hellman to include signatures and encryption

Merkle-Hellman Knapsack
- Having set of items with fixed weights
- Determining which items can be added in order to obtain a given total weight
- Illustrated using Super increasing weights (all weights greater than sum of previous)

Elliptic Curve
- Elliptic curve discrete logarithm are hard to compute than general discrete logarithm
- Smaller key size same level of security
- Elliptic curve key of 160 bits = RSA of 1024 bits
- Suited to smart cards and wireless devices (less memory and processing)
- Digital signatures, encryption and key management

Public Key Cryptosystem Algorithms
- Factoring of Large Prime Numbers
  - RSA
- Finding the discrete logarithm in a finite field
  - El Gamal
  - Diffie-Hellman
  - Shnorrs signature Algorithm
  - Elliptic Curve
  - Nybergrueppels signature algorithm

Asymmetric and Symmetric Key Comparisons

Asymmetric Key	Symmetric Key
512 bits	64 bits
1792 bits	112 bits
2304 bits	128 bits

Purpose of Digital Signatures
- To detect unauthorized modifications and to authenticate identity and non-repudiation.
- Generates block of data smaller than the original data
- One way hash functions
  - One way has produces fixed size output (digest)
  - No two messages will have same digest
  - One way no getting original file from hash
  - Message digest should be calculated using all of original files data

- After message digest is calculated it is encrypted with senders private key
- Receiver decrypts using senders public key, if it opens then it is from the sender.
- Then receiver computes message digest of sent file if hash is the same it has not been modified

Digital Signal Standard (DSS) and Secure Hash Standard (SHS)
- Enables use of RSA digital signature algorithm or DSA –Digital Signature Algorithm (based on El Gamal)
- Both use The Secure Hash Algorithm to compute message digest then processed by DSA to verify the signature. Message digest is used instead of the longer message because faster.

SHA-1 - Secure Hash Algorithm produces 160 bit digest if message is less than 2^{64} bits.
- It is computationally infeasible to find message from message digest
- It is computationally infeasible to find to different messages with same message digest
- Padding bits are added to message to make it a multiple of 512

MD5
- Developed by Ronald Rivest in 1991
- Produces 128 bit message digest

Hashed Message Authentication Code (HMAC)
- Uses key to generate a Message Authentication Code which is used as a checksum

Birthday Attack
- You in a room with better than 50/50 chance of another person having your birthday? Need 253 people
- You in a room with better than 50/50 chance of two people having the same birthday? Need 23 people

Cryptographic Attack

Brute Force Attack - try every possible combination
Known Plain Text – attacker has copy of plain text and the associated ciphertext of several messages
Chosen Plain Text – chosen plain text is encrypted. The attacker has the plaintext and ciphertext and can choose the plaintext that gets encrypted.
Adaptive Chosen Plain Text – selection of plain text is altered based on previous results
Ciphertext Only – only ciphertext is known. The attacker has the ciphertext of several messages. Each of the messages has been encrypted using the same encryption algorithm.
Chosen Ciphertext – Portions of the cipher text are selected for trial decryption while having access to plain text. The attacker can choose the ciphertext to be decrypted and has access to the resulting decrypted plaintext.
Adaptive Chosen Ciphertext - Chosen cipher text are selected for trial decryption where selection is based on previous results
Birthday Attack – the probability of two different messages having same message digest or finding two different messages that have the same message digest
Meet in the Middle – For attacking double encryption from each end and comparing in the middle
Man in the Middle – intercepting messages and forwarding on modified versions
Differential Cryptanalysis – Private key cryptography looking at text pairs after encryption looking for differences
Linear Cryptanalysis – using plain text and cipher text to generate a linear approximation of a portion of the key
Differential Linear Cryptanalysis – using both linear and differential approaches
Factoring – using mathematics to determine the prime factors of large numbers
Statistical – exploiting the lack of randomness in key generation

Public Key Certification Systems
- A source could post a public key under the name of another individual
- Digital certificates counter this attack, a certificate can bind individuals to their key
- A Certificate Authority (CA) acts as a notary to bind the key to the person
- CA must be cross-certified by another CA

Public Key Infrastructure - (PKI)
Integration of digital signatures and certificates.
- Digital Certificates
- Certificate Authorities (CA)
- Registrations Authorities
- Policies and procedures
- Certificate Revocation
- Non-repudiation support
- Timestamping
- Lightweight Directory Access Protocol
- Security Enabled Applications
- Cross Certification

Approaches to Escrowed Encryption
- Allowing law enforcement to obtain the keys to view peoples encrypted data
- Escrow the key in two pieces with two trusted escrow agents
- Court order to get both pieces
- Clipper Chip – implemented in tamper proof hardware

Key Escrow using Public Key Cryptography
- Fair Cryptosystems – Sylvio Micali, MIT
- Private key is split and distributed
- Can verify each portion of the key without joining

Key Management
- Key control
- Key recovery
- Key storage
- Key retirement/destruction
- Key Change
- Key Generation
- Key theft
- Frequency of key use

E-mail Security
- Non-repudiation
- Confidentiality of messages
- Authentication of Source
- Verification of delivery
- Labeling of sensitive material
- Control Access

Secure Multipurpose Internet Mail Extensions (S/MIME)
- Adds secure services to messages in MIME format
- Provides authentication through digital signatures
- Follows Public Key Cryptography Standards (PKCS)
- Uses X.509 Signatures

MIME Object Security Services (MOSS)
- Provides flexibility by supporting different trust models
- Uses MD5, RSA Public Key and DES
- Permits identification outside of the X.509 Standard

Privacy Enhanced Mail (PEM)
- Compliant with Public Key Cryptography Standards (PKCS)
- Developed by consortium of Microsoft, Sun, and Novell
- Triple DES-EDE – Symmetric Encryption
- MD2 and MD5 Message Digest
- RSA Public Key – signatures and key distribution
- X.509 Certificates and formal CA

Pretty Good Privacy - PGP
- Phil Zimmerman
- Symmetric Cipher using IDEA
- RSA is used for signatures and key distribution
- No CA, uses "web of trust"
- Users can certify each other

Message Authentication Code
- Check value derived from message contents

SET – Secure Electronic Transaction
- Visa and Mastercard developed in 1997
- Encrypts the payment information
- DES – Symmetric Encryption
- RSA Public Key – signatures and key distribution

Secure Sockets Layer (SSL) - HTTPS
- Developed by Netscape in 1994
- Uses public key to authenticate server to the client
- Also provides option client to sever authentication
- Supports RSA public Key Algorithms, IDEA, DES, and 3DES
- Supports MD5 Hashing
- HTTPS header
- Resides between the application and TCP layer
- Can be used by telnet, FTP, HTTP and e-mail protocols.
- Based on X.509

Transaction Layer Security
- Successor to SSL

Internet Open Trading Protocol – (IOTP)
- Aimed at consumer to business transaction
- Flexible and future focused

MONDEX
- Smart cash card application
- Proprietary encryption algorithm
- Card is same as cash

IPSec
- Provides encryption, access control, and non-repudiation over IP.
- Two Main Protocols are
  - Authentication Header – integrity, authentication and non-repudiation
  - Encapsulating Security Payload – encryption, limited authentication

- Security Association is required between two parties – one way connection - Comprised of Security Parameter Index – (SPI) – 32 bit identifier
- Bi-directional communication requires two Security Associations

- In VPN implementation IPSec can operate in transport or tunnel mode
  - Tunnel mode – data and original IP header encrypted, new header is added
  - Transport mode – data encrypted, header not
  - New header has address of VPN gateway
  - MD5 and SHA are used for integrity
  - Security Associations can be combined into bundles using either
    - Transport Adjacency
    - Iterated Tunneling
- **IKE – Internet Key Exchange is used for key management with IPSEC**
- IKE is set of three protocols:
  - Internet Security and Key Management Protocol (ISAKMP) –phases for establishing relationship
  - Secure Key Exchange Mechanism – SKEME – secure exchange mechanism
  - Oakley – modes of operation needed to establish secure connection

S/WAN – Secure WAN – defines IPSec based widespread use of VPNs on the internet

S-HTTP – Alternative to SSL
- Can be used to secure individual WWW Documents
- SSL is session based

Secure Shell – SSH-2
- Remote access via encrypted tunnel
- Client to server authentication
- Comprised of:
  - Transport Layer protocol
  - User Authentication protocol
  - Connection Protocol

Wireless Security
WAP – Wireless Application Protocol
Designed for mobile devices (PDA, Phones)
Set of protocols covering layers 7 to 3 of the OSI model
Less overhead than TCP/IP
- Wireless Markup language (WML)
- Wireless Application Environment (WAE)
- Wireless Session Protocol (WSP)
- Wireless Transport Security Protocol (WTLS)
- Wireless Datagram Protocol (WDP)

For security WAP uses Wireless Transport Security Protocol (WTLS)
Three classes of security
- Class 1 – Anonymous Authentication
- Class 2- Sever Authentication
- Class 3 – Two way client and server authentication

Security vulnerability of WAP
- WAP GAP – where WTLS is decrypted and re-encrypted to SSL at the WAP gateway

C-HTML is competing with WML from Japan
C-HTML is stripped down HTML, C-HTML can be displayed on standard browser

IEEE – 802.11 Standards
- Interface between clients and base station
- 802.11 Layers
- The physical layer PHY can use:
  - DSSS - Direct Sequence Spread Spectrum
  - FH – Frequency Hoping Spread Spectrum
  - IR – Infrared pulse modulation
- MAC Layer – Medium Access Control
- Specifies CSMA/CA Carrier Sense Multiple Access Collision Avoidance
- Provides:
- Data Transfer
- Association
- Re-association
- Authentication - WEP
- Privacy - WEP
- Power Management

Domain 5 – Security Architecture and Models

Computer Architecture - Organization of the fundamental elements comprising the computer

Main components
- CPU – Central Processing Unit
- Memory
- Input / Output devices

Arithmetic Logic Unit - CPU contains ALU performs arithmetic and logical operations on binary

Computer elements connected via a group of conductors called the BUS
- Address Bus
- Data Bus
- Control Bus

Memory

Cache Memory
- Small amount of very high speed RAM
- Holds instruction and data from primary memory that is likely to be used in the current operation, increases apparent RAM access time

Random Access Memory
- Memory where locations can be directly addressed and the data that is stored can be altered.
- RAM is volatile – lose power = lose data
- DRAM – Dynamic RAM
    - data is stored in parasitic capacitance and needs to be refreshed – read and rewritten every few milliseconds
    - Multi-phase clock signals used
- SRAM – Static RAM
    - Uses latches to store the bits does not need refreshing
    - Single-phase clock signals used

Programmable Logic Device
- Integrated circuit with connections or internal logic gates that can be changed through programming
- Examples of PLD
    - ROM – Read Only Memory
    - PAL – Programmable Array Logic

ROM - Read Only Memory
- Non-volatile storage where locations can be directly addressed
- Data can not be altered dynamically
- Data remains when power is lost
- Some ROMs can not be altered
- Other Flash type memories can be altered but slow data transfer compared to other types of memory
    - EPROMS – Erasable Programmable Read Only Memories
    - EEPROMS – Electrically Erasable Programmable Read Only Memories
- Infrequent changes
- AKA - firmware

Real or Primary Memory
- Directly addressable by the CPU
- Usually RAM

Secondary Memory
- Non-volatile
- Slower
- Example Magnetic Disks

Sequential Memory
- Must be searched from beginning
- Example – Magnetic Tape Drive

Virtual Memory
- Uses secondary memory in conjunction with primary memory to present the CPU with more virtual primary memory

Addressing Modules – CPU uses to address memory
- Register Addressing – Addressing registers within the CPU or registers in the primary memory
- Direct Addressing – Addressing a portion of primary memory with actual address of the memory
- Absolute Addressing – addressing all of the primary memory space
- Indexed Addressing – adding the memory address to and index register to then address memory location
- Implied Addressing – Internal register no need to supply the address
- Indirect Addressing – address specified in the instruction contains final desired location

Memory protection – means to prevent one program from modifying the memory contents of another. Implemented by the Operating System or the Hardware.

Instruction Execution Cycle
Two Phases
- **Fetch**
  - CPU presents address of the instruction to memory
  - Retrieves instructions located at that address
- **Execute**
  - Instruction is decoded and executed
- Controlled by the CPU clock signals
  - Multi-Phase clock signals used for DRAM
  - Single Phase clock signals used for SRAM
- Some instructions require more than one machine cycle to execute
- Different States of Operation:
  - Run or operating state
  - Application or problem state
    - Non-privileged instruction – subset of instructions for user
  - Supervisory State
    - Privileged instructions – System Administrator may execute
  - Wait State - accessing slow memory

Modern Computer Enhancements

- **Pipelining** – increases performance by overlapping the steps of instructions
  - Three Phases - Fetch – Decode – Execute
- **Complex Instruction Set** – instructions perform many operations per instruction, based on taking advantage of longer fetch times
- **Reduced Instruction Set** - simpler instruction that require less clock cycles to complete
  - Result of faster processors that enabled the fetch process to be done as quickly as decode and Execute
- **Scalar Processor** – processor that executes one instruction at a time
- **Superscalar Processor** – processor that enables concurrent execution of multiple instructions in the same pipeline

- **Very Long Instruction Word Processor – VLIW** – processor in which a single instruction specifies more than one concurrent operation
- **Multiprogramming** – Executes two or more programs simultaneously on a single processor
- **Multitasking** – Executes two or more subprograms at the same time on a single processor
- **Multiprocessor** – Executes two or more programs at the same time on multiple processors

Input / Output Structures
- A processor communicates with outside devices through (I/O) interface adapters
- Complex provide
  - Data buffering
  - Timing and interrupt controls
- Adapters have addresses on the computer bus
- If the adapter has address in the memory space it is known on memory-mapped (I/O)
  - Benefit is that CPU sees adapter as any other memory device

Types of I/O:
- Block devices (write blocks of data; hard disk)
- Character devices (not addressable; keyboard and printer)

CPU operating states: ready state, problem state, supervisory state, and wait state

Direct Memory Access – DMA
Data is transferred directly to and from the memory bypassing the CPU

Interrupt Processing – an external signal interrupts the normal program flow and requests service, when the service is complete the CPU restores the state of the original program, CPU can turn off interrupts

- **Software** – Binary codes is machine language instructions
- **Assembly Language** - Mnemonics for basic instruction set specific to the computer
  - One to one relationship for each assembly instruction to each machine instruction
- **Source code** - assembly goes through assembler to become object (machine) code
- **Disassembler** will reverse machine code into assembly
- **MACRO's** can be used to represent several functions in assembly

- **High level languages** – English like statements, C, Java, Pascal FORTAN, BASIC

- High level code is compiled in compiler or interpreter into machine code
  - Compiler – FORTAN, C, Java
  - Interpreter – Java, BASIC

Generation Language (GL) 1GL (machine), 2GL (assembly), 3-5 GL (High level)
- 1 GL – machine language: **Assembler** – translates from assembly language to machine language.
- 2 GL – assembly language: **Disassembler** – translates machine language to assembly.
- 3 GL – Fortran, BASIC, C languages: **Compiler** – translates high-level language to machine code.
- 4 GL – NATURAL, FOCUS, and database query languages: **Decompiler** – translates machine language into high-level language.
- 5GL – Prolog, LISP and other Artificial Intelligence languages: **Interpreter** – translates high-level language one command at time to machine code.

Operating System (OS)– program or set of programs that controls the resources and operations of the computer

Controller - OS communicates with I/O through controller (i.e. disk controller)

Open systems – published specifications, subject to open review and evaluation, vulnerabilities exposed during review.

Closed systems – vendor proprietary usually not compatible with other systems, no open review, may have unexposed vulnerabilities

Distributed Computing

Migration from central computing to the client server model, including desktops.
Major concerns:

- Desktops can contain sensitive information but are at risk
- Users lack general security awareness
- Desktop can provide an avenue of access into other critical systems
- Modems can make the network vulnerable
- Downloading data from the Internet increases risk of infection with malicious code
- Desktop may not be physically secure
- Lack of backups on desktop

Security Mechanisms

- E-mail and download policies
- Robust Access control, including biometrics at the desktop
- GUI access to restrict access to critical information
- File encryption
- Separation of the processes that run in privileged mode
- Protection of domains
- Protection of sensitive disks with physical security
- Distinct labeling according tom classification
- Centralized backup of desktop files
- Regular security awareness training
- Control of software installed on desktops
- Encryption and hash totals for use in sending information
- Logging of transactions and transmissions
- Application of other physical, logical and administrative access controls
- DBMS systems that restrict access to data
- Protection against environmental damage
- Formal change management and development and implementations
- Desktops included in DR and BCP plans

Protection Mechanisms

- **Protection Domain** - Execution of memory space assigned to each process
    - Protects from unauthorized modification and executional interference

- **Trusted Computing Base** – Total Combination of protection mechanisms
    - Hardware
    - Software
    - Firmware
- **Security perimeter** - separates TCB from the rest of the system

- **Trusted Path** - must exist for user to gain protected access to the TCB

Protection Rings

- **Ring 0** - Most privileged domain is in the middle ring 0, usually the OS Kernel
- **Security Kernel** - is hardware, firmware and software (TCB) that implements the Reference Monitor
- **Reference Monitor** – a system component that enforces access control of an object
- **Reference Monitor Concept** - an abstract machine that mediates all access of subjects to objects
- **Security Kernel must**
    - Mediate all access
    - Be protected from modification
    - Be verified as correct

- Access rights decrease as rings increase, according to least privilege
- Ring system implemented by MIT in MULTICS designed 64 rings, in practice 8 rings were used

Other Approaches
- Using separate hardware
- Using virtual machines on the same machine with different levels of security
- Using a software security kernel that has its own hardware protection domain

Security Labels
- Assigned to a resource to indicate classification level
- Usually not changed
- Effective access control mechanism
- Require additional overhead for verification

Security Modes
Systems operate in different modes based on the level of classification and clearance of the users
- **High Mode of Operation** – **all** users have a security **clearance** or authorization to access the information but **not** necessarily a **need-to-know** for all the information processed on the system (only some of the data).
- **Multi Level Operation** - **Permits two or more classification levels** of information to be processed at the **same time** when all the users do **not** have the clearance of formal approval **to access all** the information being processed by the system
- **Dedicated** – **all** users have the **clearance** or authorization and **need-to-know** to all data processed within the system.
- **Compartmented** – **all** users have the **clearance** to access all the information processed by the system, but might **not** have the **need-to-know** and formal access approval.
- **Controlled** – type of multilevel security limited level of trust in the systems hardware/software
- **Limited Access** – minimum level of clearance is uncleared (no clearance) and sensitive but unclassified data

Additional Considerations
- **Covert Channel** – Unintended communication path between two resources that allows transfer of information in violation of security policy
- **Lack of Parameter Checking** – Failure to check the size of input streams, Can allow Buffer Overflow
- **Maintenance Hook** – (trapdoor) allows maintenance of system bypassing security
- **Time of Check to Time of Use** – attack that exploits the difference in time between time security applied and time that service is used

Recovery Procedures
- Failure must not compromise the security of the system
- If system restart is required it must re-start in safe mode (maintenance mode)
- **Maintenance Mode** - allows access only by privileged users
- **Fault Tolerance** – allows component of system to fail and recover
- **Fail Safe System** – processing is halted if component of system fails
- **Fail Soft (resilient)** – non critical processing is halted if component of system fails
- **Failover** – switching to duplicate or "hot" backup
- **Cold Start** – when the TCB and software may be inconsistent and outside intervention is required

Assurance
- Degree of confidence in satisfaction of security needs

Evaluation Criteria
- **Trusted Computer Security Evaluation Criteria** – (TCSEC) was developed in 1985 by National Computer Security Center (NCSC)

TCSEC Provides the following:
- Basis for establishing security requirements in the acquisition specifications

- Standard of security services that should be provided by the vendor
- Means to measure trustworthiness of an information system

TCSEC is the Orange Book – part of rainbow series
- Basic control objectives of Orange Book:
    - Security Policy
    - Assurance
    - Accountability

Orange Book Addresses:
- Confidentiality
- **NOT** Integrity
- It looks specifically at the operating system and not other issues

Levels
D – Minimal Protection
C – Discretionary Protection – (C1 and C2)
B – Mandatory Protection – (B1, B2, and B3)
A – Verified protection, formal methods (A1)

Trusted Network Interpretation (TNI)– Red Book
- Addresses confidentiality and integrity in trusted computer/communications network systems

Trusted Database Management System Interpretation – (TDI)
- Addresses trusted database management systems

European Information Technology Security Evaluation Criteria (ITSEC)
- Addresses confidentiality and integrity and availability
- Target of Evaluation (TOE) – system to be evaluated
    - TOE must have a security target – including security enforcing mechanisms and security policy
- Separately evaluates functionality and assurance
    - Ten Functionality Classes - F
    - Eight Assurance Levels - Q
    - Seven Levels of Correctness – E
    - Eight basic security functions
    - Listed as F-X, E

European ITSEC	TCSEC
F-C1, E1	C1
F-C2, E2	C2
F-B1, E3	B1
F-B2, E4	B2
F-B3, E5	B3
F-B3, E6	A1

Other Classes of ITSEC address high integrity and high availability

Common Criteria
- TCSEC, ITSEC and Canadian Trusted Computer Product Evaluation Criteria (CTCPEC) have evolved into one common criteria
- Common Criteria defines Protection Profile that specifies the security requirements and protections of the product to be evaluated.
- Organized around TCB entities
    - Physical and logical controls
    - Start up and recovery
    - Reference mediation
    - Privileged States

Certification and Accreditation
- Formal methods to ensure that appropriate safeguards are in place and functioning per the specifications
- Must be regularly checked after a defined period of time

Certification – evaluation of technical and non-technical security features to establish how the design meets the security requirements

Accreditation – A formal declaration by a Designated Approving Authority (DAA) where a system is approved to operate in a security mode

US Defense and Government Accreditation and Certification Standards
DITSCAP – Defense Information Technology Security Certification Accreditation Process
NIACAP - National Information Assurance Certification Accreditation Process

DITSCAP – Defense Information Technology Security Certification Accreditation Process
Establishes a standard process, a set activities, general task descriptions and a management structure to certify and accredit system will maintain its required security posture.
Four Phases of DITSCAP
- Definition – understanding of environment and architecture
- Verification – Verify compliance with System Security Authorization (While evolving)
- Validation - Validate compliance with System Security Authorization (final)
- Post Accreditation – continuing operation

NIACAP - National Information Assurance Certification Accreditation Process
- Minimum national standards for accrediting national security system
- Establishes a standard process, a set activities, general task descriptions and a management structure to certify and accredit system will maintain its required security posture.
Three types of NIACAP accreditation
- Site accreditation – evaluates application at self contained location
- Type accreditation – evaluates application at number of locations
- System accreditation - evaluates a major application or support system

Information Security Models
- Access control models
- Integrity Models
- Information Flow Models

Access Control Models
Access Matrix
Take-Grant
Bell-Lapadula Confidentiality
State Machine

Access Matrix
Straight Forward provides access rights to subjects for objects.
- Access Rights – Read, write and execute
- Subject – can be a person or a program
- Objects – file or storage device
- Columns - are called Access Control Lists
- Rows - are capability lists
- Supports Discretionary Access Control
- **Triple** - Subjects capability is defined by a triple (object, rights, random#)
  - The random number prevents spoofing

Take-Grant Model
Uses a directed graph to specify the rights a subject can transfer to an object or take from another subject.

Bell-Lapadula – confidentiality model
- Developed to formalize the US Department of Defense multilevel security policy
- Only deals with confidentiality does not deal with integrity or availability
- Based on Government Classification – Unclassified, Sensitive But Unclassified (SBU), Confidential, Secret, Top Secret
- Must have need to know
- A Trusted Subject can violate the *property
- Does not address client/server model
- Based on State Machine Concept
- Starts at secure state and transitions from one state to another.
  - The initial state must be secure and the transitions result in a secure state

Bell-Lapadula Security State Defined by three properties:
1. Simple Security Property (ss Property) – no reading from lower subject to higher object (No Read Up)
2. The * (star) security Property – No writing from higher subject to lower object (No write Down)
   - Trusted Subject can violate the star property but not its intent
   - Strong * property – no reading or writing to another level
3. Discretionary Security Property – Uses Access Matrix to specify discretionary access control

Discretionary access can be:
- Content Dependent – access decisions based on data contained in the object data.
- Context Dependent – access based on subject or object attributes to make these decisions (i.e. job role, earlier accesses, and file creation dates and times).

Weaknesses of Bell-Lapadula
- Does not address covert channels
- Does not address modern systems that use file sharing and server
- Does not define secure state transition
- Based on multilevel security does not address other policy types

Integrity Models

Biba Integrity Model
Integrity defined by three goals
- Data protected from modification by unauthorized users
- Data protected from unauthorized modification by authorized users
- Data is internally and externally consistent.

Biba Integrity Model
- Developed in 1977 as an integrity add on to Bell-Lapadula
- Lattice Based uses less than or equal to relation
- A lattice structure is a set with a least upper bound (LUB) and a greatest lower bound (GLB)
- Lattice represents a set of integrity classes (IC) and an ordered relationship
- Lattice = (IC, $\leq$, LUB, GUB)

Integrity Axioms
1. The Simple Integrity Axiom - no reading of lower object from higher subject (No Read Down)
2. The * (star) Integrity Axiom – No writing from lower subject to higher object (No write Up)
3. A subject at a lower level of integrity can not invoke a subject at a higher level of integrity

Clark-Wilson Integrity Model
- **Two elements:** well formed transaction and separation of duties.
- Developed in 1987 for use in real-world commercial environment

- Addresses the three integrity goals
- Constrained Data Item (CDI) – A data Item whose integrity is to be preserved
- Integrity Verification Procedure (IVP) – confirms that all CDIs have integrity
- Transformation Procedure (TP) – transforms a CDI from one integrity state to another integrity state
- Unconstrained Data Item – data items outside of the control area of the modeled environment
- Requires Integrity Labels

Information Flow Models
- Each object and subject is assigned security class and value; info is constrained to flow in directions that are permitted by the security policy.
- Based on state machine and consists of objects, state transitions and lattice (flow policy) states.
- Object can be a user
- Each object is assigned a security class and value
- Information is constrained to flow in the directions permitted by the policy

Non-interference Model
Actions of group A using commands C are not seen by users in Group B using commands D

Composition Theories
When smaller systems are combined they must maintain the component system security properties

McClean – defined internal and external compositional constructions
- External Constructs
  - Cascading – one systems input is the output of another
  - Feedback – one systems output is input to another system and returned as input to the first system
  - Hookup – a system that communicates with another system and external entities
- Internal Constructs:
  - Intersection, Union and Difference

Conclusion – security maintained in cascading constructs but subject to other system variables for other constructs

Orange Book – Trusted Computer Security Evaluation Criteria
- (TCSEC) was developed in 1985 by National Computer Security Center (NCSC)

- **D – Minimal protection**
  - Evaluated but fail to meet requirements

- **C – Discretionary Access Control**
  - **C1 – Discretionary Security Protection**
    - Nominally satisfies discretionary controls
  - **C2 – Controlled Access protection**
    - Users accountability - through login and auditing

- **B – Mandatory Access Control**
  - **B1 – Labeled Security**
    - Data labeling
    - Informal security policy model
  - **B2 – Structured**
    - Trusted Facility Management - Support Operator and Security Administrator
    - Covert Channel – Covert Storage Channels
    - Configuration Change Management – Development and Maintenance
  - **B3- Security Domains**
    - Trusted Facility Management – Identify Security Administrator Functions
    - Covert Channel – Covert Storage and Covert Timing Channels
    - Trusted Recovery Required
    - Configuration Change Management – Development and Maintenance

- **A – Verified Design**
  - **A1 – Verified Design**
    - Trusted Facility Management – Identify Security Administrator Functions
    - Covert Channel – Covert Storage and Covert Timing Channels
    - Trusted Recovery Required
    - Configuration Change Management – Entire System Lifecycle

European ITSEC	TCSEC	Common Criteria
E0	D	EAL1
F-C1, E1	C1	EAL2
F-C2, E2	C2	EAL3
F-B1, E3	B1	EAL4
F-B2, E4	B2	EAL5
F-B3, E5	B3	EAL6
F-B3, E6	A1	EAL7

Domain 6 – Operations Security

Triples
- **Threat** – an event that could cause harm by violating the security (i.e. Operator abuse of privileges)
- **Vulnerability** – weakness in a system that enables security to be violated (i.e. Weak Segregation of duties)
- **Asset** – anything that is a computer resource (i.e. software data)

C.I.A.
- **Confidentiality** – operations controls affect confidentiality of data.
- **Integrity** – how well operations controls are implemented affects data integrity
- **Availability** – fault tolerance and ability to recover

Controls and protections
Controls to protect hardware, software and media from:
- Threats in an operating environment
- Internal and external intruders
- Operators inappropriately accessing resources

Categories of Controls
- **Preventative** – prevent harmful occurrence
  - Lower amount and impact of errors entering the system
  - Prevent unauthorized intruders from accessing the system
- **Detective** – detect after harmful occurrence
  - Track unauthorized transactions
- **Corrective** – restore after harmful occurrence
  - Data recovery

Additional Control Categories
- **Deterrent Control** – encourage compliance with external controls
- **Application Controls** – designed into software applications
- **Transaction Controls** – control over the various stages of a transaction
- **Input Controls** – ensure transactions properly input
- **Processing Controls** – guarantee transactions are proper and valid
- **Output Controls** – protect the confidentiality and integrity of output
- **Change Controls** – preserve integrity when configuration changes are made
- **Test Controls** – ensure data integrity and confidentiality of data during testing

Orange Book Controls – TCSEC – Trusted Computer Security Evaluation Criteria
Assurance – level of confidence that security policies have been implemented correctly

Operational Assurance – focuses on basic features and architecture of a system
- System Architecture
- System Integrity
- **Covert Channel Analysis**
- **Trusted Facility Management**
- **Trusted Recovery**

Life Cycle Assurance – controls and standards required for building and maintaining a system
- Security Testing
- Design Specification and testing
- **Configuration Management**
- Trusted Distribution

Covert Channel Analysis
- An information path that is not normally within a system and is therefore not protected by the systems' normal security mechanism.
- Secret ways to convey information to another program or person
  - **Covert Storage Channels** - convey information by changing stored data **(B2)**

  - **Covert Timing Channels** – convey information by altering the performance of or modifying the timing of system resources in measurable way. **(B3, A1= Storage and Timing)**

Combat Covert Channel Analysis - with noise and traffic generation

Trusted Facility Management - Required for **B2, B3, and A1**
- Defined as assignment of a specific individual to administer the security of a system. (Security Administrator)

Separation of Duties
- Assign different tasks to different personnel
- No single person can completely compromise a system
- Related to the concept of least privileges – least privileges required to do one's job

- Secure Systems - System Administrator and Security Administrator must be different roles.
- Highly Secure Systems - System Administrator, Security Administrator, and Enhanced Operator must be different roles.
- If same person roles must be controlled and audited.

System Admin – Enhanced Operator Functions
- Installing software
- Start up and shut down of system
- Adding removing users
- Performing back up and recovery
- Handling printers and queues

Security Administrator Functions
- Setting user clearances, initial passwords and other security characteristics for new users
- Changing security profiles for users
- Setting file sensitivity labels
- Setting security of devices
- Renewing audit data

- **B2** security level requires that systems must support separate operator and system administrator roles.
- **B3 and A1**, systems must clearly identify the functions of the security administrator to perform the security-related functions.

Rotation of duties
Limiting the length of time a person performs duties before being moved

Trusted Recovery - Required for B3 and A1 levels
- Ensures Security is not breached when a system crashes or fails
- System must be restarted without compromising security
- Two primary activities
  - Failure Preparation –
    - Backups on a regular basis
  - System Recovery -
    - Rebooting in single user mode – no other users allowed on the system
    - Recovering all file systems
    - Restoring files

- Recovering security
- Checking security critical files

Three hierarchical recovery types:
- Manual Recovery – Sys Admin must be involved
- Automated Recovery – no intervention for single failure
- Automated Recovery without Undue Loss – similar to Automated Recovery, higher level pf recovery no undue loss of protected object

Configuration Change Management – Required B2, B3 and A1
- Process of tracking and approving changes
- Identify, control and audit changes
- Changes to the system must not diminish security
- Includes roll back procedures
- Documentation updates to reflect changes
- Recommended for systems below the required B2, B3 and A1
- Change Control Functions:
    - Orderly manner and formalized testing
    - Users informed of changes
    - Analyze effects of changes
    - Reduce negative impact of changes
- Configuration Management required for Development and Implementation stages for **B2 and B3**
- Configuration Management required for life cycle of system for **A1**

Administrative Controls
- HR and personnel controls
- Personnel Security –
- Employment screening
- Mandatory Vacation
- Warnings and Termination for violating security policy
- Separation of Duties
- Least Privileges
- Need to Know
- Change Control/ Configuration Control
- Record Retention and Documentation

Least privilege
- No access beyond job requirements
- Group level privileges for Operators
    - Read Only
    - Read /Write - usually copies of original data
    - Access Change – make changes to original data

Operations Jobs
- Computer Operator – backups, system console, mounting tapes, hardware, software
- Operations Analyst – works with application developers, maintenance programmers and computer operators
- Job Control Analyst – responsible for overall job control quality
- Production Scheduler – planning and timing of processing
- Production Control Analyst – printing and distribution of reports
- Tape Librarian – collects tapes, manages off-site storage

Record Retention - Records should be maintained according to management, legal, audit and tax requirements

Data Remanence – Data left on media after it has been erased

Due care and Due Diligence – Security Awareness, Signed Acceptance of Employee Computer Use Policy

Documentation – procedures for operations, contingency plans, security polices and procedures

Operation Controls

Resource Protection
- Protecting Resources from disclosure alteration or misuse
  - Hardware – routers, firewalls, computers, printers
  - Software – libraries, vendor software, OS software
  - Data Resource – backup data, user data, logs

Hardware Controls
- Hardware Maintenance
  - Requires physical and logical access by support and vendors
  - Supervision of vendors and maintenance, background checks
- Maintenance Accounts
  - Disable maintenance accounts when not needed
  - Rename default passwords
- Diagnostic Port Control
  - Specific ports for maintenance
  - Should be blocked from external access
- Hardware Physical Controls – require locks and alarms
  - Sensitive operator terminals
  - Media storage rooms
  - Server and communications equipment
  - Modem pools and circuit rooms

Software Controls
- Anti-virus Management – prevent download of viruses
- Software Testing – formal rigid software testing process
- Software Utilities – control of powerful utilities
- Safe software Storage – prevent modification of software and copies of backups
- Back up Controls – test and restore backups

Privileged Entity Controls –" privileged operations functions"
- Extended special access to system commands
- Access to special parameters
- Access to system control program – some only run in particular state

Media Resource Protection

Media Security Controls – prevent the loss of sensitive information when the media is stored outside the system
- Logging – log the use of the media, provides accountability
- Access Control – physical access control
- Proper Disposal – sanitization of data – rewriting, degaussing, destruction

Media Viability Controls – protect during handling, shipping and storage
- Marking – label and mark media, bar codes
- Handling – physical protection of data
- Storage – security and environmental protection from heat, humidity, liquids, dust, smoke, magnetism

Physical Protection
Protection from physical access
- Hardware – routers, firewalls, computers, printers
- Software – libraries, vendor software, OS software

Physical piggybacking – following an authorized person through a door

Monitoring and Auditing
Monitoring – problem identification and resolution
Monitor for:
- Illegal Software Installation
- Hardware Faults
- Error States
- Operational Events

Penetration Testing – Testing a networks defenses by using the same techniques as external intruders
- Scanning and Probing – port scanners
- Demon Dialing – war dialing for modems
- Sniffing – capture data packets
- Dumpster Diving – searching paper disposal areas
- Social Engineering – most common, get information by asking

Violation Analysis
- Clipping levels must be established to be effective
- Clipping Level – baseline of normal activity, used to ignore normal user errors
- Profile Based Anomaly Detection
- Looking for:
    - Repetitive Mistakes
    - Individuals who exceed authority
    - Too many people with unrestricted access
    - Patterns indication serious intrusion attempts

Auditing
IT Auditors Audit:
- Backup Controls
- System and Transaction Controls
- Data Library Controls
- Systems Development Standards
- Data Center Security
- Contingency Plans

Audit Trails
- Enables tracking of history of modifications, deletions, additions.
- Allow for accountability
- Audit logs should record:
    - Transaction time and date
    - Who processed transaction
    - Which terminal was used
    - Various security events relating to transaction

Also should look at:
- Amendment to production jobs
- Production job reruns
- Computer Operator practices

Other issues with audit logs:
Retention and Protection of audit media and reports
Protection against alteration

Problem Management
Goals of problem management:
- Reduce failures to a manageable level
- Prevent occurrence of a problem
- Mitigate the impact of problems

Potential Problems:
- Performance and availability of computing resources
- The system and networking infrastructure
- Procedures and transactions
- Safety and security of personnel

Abnormal Events - that can be discovered by an audit
- Degraded resource availability
- Deviations from the standard transaction procedures
- Unexplained occurrences in a processing chain

Objective of problem management is resolution of the problem

Threats and Vulnerabilities
Threat - if realized can cause damage to a system or create a loss of C.I.A.
Vulnerability – a weakness in a system that can be exploited by a threat

Threats:
Accidental loss
Operator input error and omissions - manual input errors
Transaction processing errors – programming errors

Inappropriate Activities:
- Can be grounds for job action or dismissal
- Inappropriate content – storing inappropriate content like porn
- Waste of Corporate Resources – personal use of hardware and software
- Sexual or Racial Harassment – Using e-mail or other resources to distribute inappropriate material
- Abuse of privileges or rights – using unauthorized access levels to violate confidentiality of company data

Illegal Computer Operations
- Eavesdropping – sniffing, dumpster diving, social engineering
- Fraud – collusion, falsified transactions
- Theft – information or trade secrets, physical hardware and software theft
- Sabotage – Denial of Service (DoS), production delays
- External Attacks – malicious cracking, scanning, war dialing

Vulnerabilities
- Traffic/Trend Analysis – analyzing data characteristics
- Countermeasures include:
  - Padding Messages – making messages uniform size
  - Sending Noise – transmitting non-informational data elements to disguise real data
- Covert Channel Analysis – unintended channel

Data Scavenging
- Piecing together information from bits of data
  - Keyboard Attacks – sitting at the keyboard using normal utilities to gain information
  - Laboratory Attack – using very precise electronic equipment

IPL Vulnerabilities – Initial Program Load
- Ability to put the system in single user mode at boot up
- Grants Operator powerful features

Network Address Hijacking
- Enables intruder to capture traffic for analysis or password theft
- Intruder can reroute the data output, obtain supervisory terminal function and bypass system logs.

Domain 7 – Applications and System Development

Software Development Lifecycle
- Goals:
  - Produce Quality product that meets users needs
  - Stay within budget and time schedule

Simplistic Model
Took into account each stage but did not take into account any rework that may be required by later stages

Waterfall Model
- Allows developer to go back and work on the previous stage
- Limited to one stage back
- Fundamental problem:
  - Assumes that a stage will finish at a specific time
  - Usually not the case in the real world
  - If an ending phase is forcibly tied to a milestone, the milestone can not be considered met until the rework is concluded
  - In 1976 Barry Boehm, reworked waterfall model to have all phases end with a Milestone and the back references represents *verification and validation* against baselines

Verification – evaluates the product against the specification

Validation – evaluates the product against the real world requirements

Waterfall Model: *System Requirements→Software Requirements→Analysis→Program Design→Coding→Testing→Operations & Maintenance*

The Spiral Model
- Developed in 1988 by Barry Boehm
- Incorporates the various phases of software development
- Broken out into Quadrants
- Cost is on the radial dimension (Y – Axis)
- Quadrants:
  - Lower Left – Developing Plans
  - Upper Left – Defines Objectives
  - Upper Right – Prototyping to identify risks
  - Lower Right – Final Development
- Left Horizontal Axis represents major review to complete each full cycle

Information Security and the Life Cycle Model
- Information Security: controls conception, development, implementation, testing, and maintenance should be conducted concurrently with the system software life cycle phases

Testing Issues
- Unit testing should be addressed when modules are designed
- Personnel separate from the developers should test
- Should include out of range situations
- Test cases should be used with known expected values

Software Maintenance Phase
- **Request Control – manage user requests**
  - Establish priorities
  - Estimate Costs
  - Determine interface presented to user

Change Control
- Recreating and analyzing the problem
- Developing changes and tests
- Performing quality control
- Tools to be used for changes
- Documentation of changes
- Restriction of changes' effect on other parts of code
- Recertification and accreditation

- **Release Control**
  - Issuing the latest release of the software

Configuration Management
BS 7799 – The discipline of identifying components of a continually evolving system for the purposes of controlling changes to those components maintaining integrity and traceability throughout the lifecycle.

- Configuration Item – component which is to be changed
- Version – recorded state of the configuration item
- Configuration – collection of component configuration
- Building – process of assembling a version
- Build List – set of version used to build configuration item
- Software Library – controlled area

Configuration Identification – identify and document the functional characteristics of configuration item

Configuration Control – control changes to configuration items from software library, issuing versions

Configuration Status Accounting – record the processing of changes

Configuration Audit - Control of the quality of configuration management

The Software Capability Maturity Model
- Quality of finished product is a component of the quality of the development process
- CMM developed by the Software Engineering Group (SEI) in 1986
- Defines Five Maturity Levels
  - Level 1 – Initiating – competent people, processes are informal and ad hoc
  - Level 2 – Repeatable – has project management processes
  - Level 3 – Defined – technical practices are integrated with management practices
  - Level 4 – Managed – product and processes are quantitatively controlled
  - Level 5 – Optimizing – Continuous process improvement

The Software CMM supports the concept of continuous improvement

Process Improvement IDEAL Model
Phase 1 – Initiate – begin formal process improvement effort
Phase 2 – Diagnose – Perform Assessment
Phase 3 – Establish – Develop prioritized action plan
Phase 4 – Action – implement process improvement
Phase 5 – Leverage – reassess and continuously improve

Benefits:
- Improved Software Quality
- Reduced Lifecycle
- More accurate scheduling
- Management visibility
- Proactive Planning and tracking

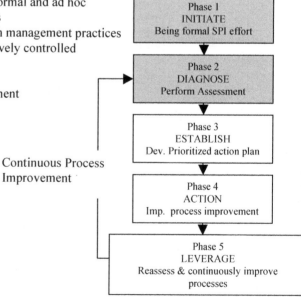

Software Development Life Cycle:

1. System Feasibility

Information Security Policy	Legal Issues
Standards	Early Validation of concepts

2. Software Plans & Requirements

Threats	Legal Liabilities
Vulnerabilities	Cost/Benefit Analysis
Security Requirements	Level of Protection Desired
Reasonable Care	Develop Test Plans
Due Diligence	Validation

3. Product Design

Incorporate Security Specifications	Design Documentation
Adjust Test Plans and Data	Evaluate Encryption Options
Determine Access Controls	Verification

4. Detailed Design

Design Security Controls Commensurate with legal requirements	Detailed Documentation Design
Design Access Controls	Consider Business Continuity Issues
Employ Encryption	Finalize User GUI
Adapt Security Test Plans	Verification

5. Coding

Develop information security-related code	Support business continuity plan
Implement unit testing	Develop documentation
Incorporate other modules or units	

6. Integration Product

Integrate Security Components	Refine Documentation
Test Integrated Modules	Conduct Security Related product verification

7. Implementation

Install Security Software	Test Security Software
Run Systems	Complete Documentation, certification, and accreditation
Conduct Acceptance Testing	

8. Operations & Maintenance

Revalidate Security controls	Deliver changes
Conduct Penetration testing and vulnerability analysis	Evaluate conformance to SLA and validations
Manage Request for Changes	Update documentation, recertification
Implement change control	

Object Oriented Systems
- Group of independent objects, cooperate to provide system's functionality
- Objects are encapsulated – can be viewed as a black box
- According to Booch, each object has a State, Behaviour, and Identity

Fundamentals of Object Oriented Systems
- **Message** – communication to an object to carry out an operation
- **Method** – the code that defines the action of the object in response to a message
- **Behavior** – results exhibited by an object in response to a message

- **Class** – collection of common objects
- **Instance** – objects are instances of classes that contain their methods
- **Inheritance** – method and class are inherited by a subclass
- **Delegation** – forwarding a request by an object to another object, no method to service the request itself
- **Polymorphism** – is objects of many different classes that are related by some common superclass; thus any object denoted by this name is able to respond to some common set of operations in a **different** way
- **Polyinstantiation** – is the development of a new version of an object from another object replacing variables with other values.
  - For example, relational database, the name of a military unit may be classified in the database and may have an ID # as the primary key. If another user at a lower classification level attempts to create a confidential entry for another unit using the same id# as a primary key, a rejection of the attempt would infer to the lower level user the same ID exists at a higher classification.
  - To avoid inference, systems will allow same id# for lower class and the DBMS would manage to permit same primary key for two different units
  - Prevents inference violations

Phases of development for object orientation:
- **Object Oriented Requirements Analysis (OORA)** – defines classes of objects and interaction
- **Object Oriented Analysis (OOA)** – understanding and modeling a problem
- **Domain Analysis (DA)** – identify objects and classes common to all application
- **Object Oriented Design (OOD)** – object is the basic unit of modularity
- **Object Oriented Programming (OOP)** – emphasizes employment of objects in programming

Reusing tested objects reduces time and testing for development

Object Request Brokers:
- Objects made available to users across networks.
- ORBs are middleware because they reside between two other entities
- Establishes client/server relationship between objects

Common Object Request Broker (CORBA) Architecture:
- Developed by Object Management Group (OMG)
- Defines industry standard enabling different programs on different platforms to communicate

Common Object Model (COM)
- Formerly known as Object Linking and Embedding (OLE)
- Support exchange of objects between programs

Distributed Common Object Model (DCOM)
Support exchange of objects across networks

Object Oriented Languages:
- Simula 67 – first Object Oriented Language
- C++
- Smalltalk

Artificial Intelligence Systems
Using software and hardware to solve problems
Two Types of AI: (Expert Systems, and Neural Networks)
Expert Systems – exhibits reasoning similar to that of a human
- Builds knowledge base (in the form of If-Then statements) of the domain to be addressed in the form of rules and an inference mechanism to determine if the rules have been satisfied by system input
- Expert System = Inference engine + knowledge base
  - Knowledge Base - contains facts and rules

- Inference Engine – compares information acquired to the knowledge base
- If there is a match the rule "fires"
- Certain rules have a higher priority – Salience

Expert Systems Operate in two modes:
Forward Chaining – acquires information and comes to a conclusion
Backward Chaining – backtracks to determine if a hypothesis is correct

Uncertainty
Bayesian Theory or "fuzzy logic"

Fuzzy Logic (addresses uncertainties)
- Degrees of uncertainty whether something is true or false
- Fuzzification – apply membership function to input variable to determine degree of truth
- Inference – truth value applied to conclusion of each rule
- Composition – all subsets combined
- Defuzzification – convert fuzzy subset to a number

Spiral Model
- Can be used to build expert system
- Acquisition of Knowledge is key
- Is a meta-model that incorporates a number of the software development models.
- Stages
  - Analysis
  - Specification
  - Development
  - Deployment
- Verification and validation – concerned with inconsistencies and conflicting rules

Neural Networks – based on functioning of biological neurons
- Neurons, signals are exchanged among neurons through electrical pulses traveling along an axon
- Electrical pulse arrives at a neuron at points called synapses
- Output = Input1*Weight1 + Input2*Weight2
- Summation of inputs with dynamic weights assigned to them
- One summing node is called a single-layer network
- Multiple summing nodes is a multi-layer network
- Training develops the weights
- Neural networks can be trained to give the correct response for each input.

Database Systems
Can be used to define, store and manipulate data without writing specific programs to perform these functions.

Different Types of Databases
- Hierarchical
- Mesh
- Object-Oriented
- Relational

Database Security Issues
- Security is provided in relational databases through views.
- Virtual relation that combines information from other relations.
- The DBMS can be compromised by circumventing the normal security controls.
- **Aggregation** – Act of obtaining information of higher sensitivity by combining information from lower levels of sensitivity.

- **Inference** – is ability of users to infer or deduce info about data at sensitivity levels for which they do not have access. A link that enables an inference to occur is called an inference channel.
- Open Database Connectivity (ODBC) – developed by Microsoft must be controlled.

Data Warehouse and Data Mining

Data Warehouse – repository of information from heterogeneous databases that is available for users to make queries.

- Data is normalized and redundant data is removed.
- Data warehouse and mining can be applied to audit logs and other info to find system anomalies.

- **Data mining:** Objective is to find relationships that were unknown up until now among data in warehouse. Searching for correlations
- **Metadata:** Correlations or data about data
- **Data mart:** Metadata is not stored in data warehouse. Metadata usually stored in a separate system.

Data Dictionary

- Database system for developers
- Records all data structures used by an application

Application Controls

Application Control Type	Accuracy	Security	Consistency
Preventative	Data Checks, custom screens, validity checks, contingency planning and backups	Firewalls, reference monitors, sensitivity labels, traffic padding, encryption, data classification, one-time passwords, separate test and development environments	Data Dictionary, programming standards, DBMS
Detective	Cyclic redundancy checks, structured walk throughs, hash totals, reasonableness checks	IDS, and audit trails	Comparison tools, relationship tests, reconciliation controls
Corrective	Backups, control reports, before and after imaging reports, checkpoint restarts	Emergency response, and reference monitor	Programs comments, database controls

Service Level Agreements

- Guarantees the level and quality of service
- Metrics in SLAs
  - Turn around times
  - Average response times
  - Number of on-line users
  - System utilization rates
  - System up times
  - Volume of transactions
  - Production problems

Distributed Systems

- Pose special challenges to security
- Security for distributed systems should include:
    - Access control
    - Identification
    - Authentication
    - Intrusion detection
    - Emergency response
    - Logs
    - Audit trails

- **Client/Server** – is a type of distributed system
- **Agent** – surrogate program performs services on behalf of another
- **Proxy** – acts on behalf of principal but may hide the principal
- **Applets** – small applications in Java or C++, mobile code
    - Applets can be downloaded from the web into a web browser. Applet can execute in the network browser
- **Java**
    - Designed to run on constrained space
    - Java is an object-oriented, distributed, interpreted (not compiled), architecture-neutral, multithreaded, general purpose programming language
- **Thread** – lightweight process
- **Interpreted language** executes one line at a time, run-time biding
- **Compiled language** is translated into machine code, binding at compile time
- **Active X** – can download mobile code in BASIC and C++
    - Establishes trust between client and server with digital certificates

Malicious Mobile Code Defenses
Ie : Java and ActiveX code downloaded into a Web browser from the WWW.
- Configure firewall to screen applets
- Configure Web Browser to restrict or prevent applets
- Configure Web Browser to restrict or prevent applets from trusted servers
- Provide user awareness training on mobile code threats

Centralized Architecture
Centralized is easier to protect than distributed.

Real Time Systems
- Operate by acquiring data from sensors and transducers in real time and make real time decisions
- Example: "Fly by wire" control of supersonic aircraft
- Availability is crucial
- Addressed through RAID – disk mirroring
- Fault Tolerant Systems – has to detect and take action to recover from faults

Others:
- **Black-box testing** observes the system external behavior.
- **White-box testing** is a detailed exam of a logical path, checking the possible conditions.
- **Compiled code** poses more risk than interpreted code because malicious code can be embedded in the compiled code and can be difficult to detect.
- **Regression testing** is the verification that what is being installed does not affect any portion of the application system already installed. It generally requires the support of automated process to repeat tests previously undertaken.
- **Code comparison** is normally used to identify the parts of the source code that have changed.
- **Integration testing** is aimed at finding bugs in the relationship and interfaces between pairs of components. It does not normally test all functions.
- **Unit testing** is the testing of a piece of code. It will only detect errors in the piece of code being tested.

Domain 8 – Business Continuity and Disaster Recovery Planning

Making the plans for recovery and putting them into action to recover with as little impact on the business as possible.

Business Continuity – ensuring the business can continue in an emergency
Disaster Recovery – recover as quickly as possible

BCP Process includes:
- Scope and Plan Initiation
- Business Impact Analysis (BIA)
- Business Continuity Plan development

DRP Process includes:
- DRP planning process
- Testing the DRP
- Disaster Recovery Procedures

Key difference between BCP and DRP - DRP addresses the procedures to be followed during and after the loss

Business Continuity Planning
- Created to prevent interruptions to normal business activity
- Protect critical business process from man made and natural disasters
- Minimize the effect and all resumption of business process

BCP Should Address:
- Local and Wide Area Networks and servers
- Telecommunications and data links
- Workstations and workspaces
- Applications software and data
- Media and records storage
- Staff duties

Number One priority is always People First!

Continuity Disruptive Events
Natural Events:
- Fires, Explosions, hazardous material spills of environmental toxins
- Earthquakes, storms, floods, and fires from nature
- Power outages and utility failures

Man Made Events:
- Bombings Sabotage
- Strikes, job actions
- Employee or Operator unavailability due to emergency evacuation
- Communications infrastructure failures

Four Prime Elements of BCP
- **Scope and Plan Initiation** – marks the beginning of BCP process
- **Business Impact Analysis** – used to help business understand the impact of a disruptive event
- **Business Continuity Plan Development** – using information from the BIA to develop the actual BCP Plan, includes testing
- **Plan Approval and Implementation** – This involves getting final management approval, creating awareness, updating as needed

Scope and Plan Initiation –
- Creating the scope
- Creating detailed account of work required
- Listing the resources to be used
- Defining management practices

Roles and Responsibilities
- BCP is enterprise wide, requires involvement from many personnel enterprise wide

BCP Committee – Responsible to create, implement and test the plan
- Made up of
  - Senior Management
  - Business Units
  - Information Systems
  - Security Administrator

Senior Managements Role
- Has ultimate responsibility for all phases of the plan
- Senior Management support is critical

Due Diligence - Stock Holders may hold Senior Management responsible as well as the Board of Directors if a disruptive event causes losses that could have been prevented with base standards of care

BCP Involvement

Who	Does What
Executive Management	Initiates project, gives final approval, gives ongoing support
Senior Business Unit Management	Identifies and prioritizes time critical systems
BCP Committee	Directs the planning, implementation and test processes
Functional Business Units	Participate in implementation and testing

Business Impact Assessment
- Helps to document what impact a disruptive event will have on the business

Vulnerability Assessment
- **Three Elements:**
  - **Criticality Prioritization** – every business unit process is identified and prioritized
  - **Downtime Estimation** – Determine Maximum Tolerable Downtime (MTD), often much shorter than expected
  - **Resource Requirements** – resource requirements for critical processes

Business Impact Analysis
- **Four Steps**
  - Gathering assessment material
  - Perform the assessment
  - Analyze the compiled information
  - Document the results

Gathering assessment material
- Org Chart to determine functional relationships
- Examine Business Success Factors, priorities and alternate processing

The Vulnerability Assessment
- Often part of the BIA, similar to risk assessment, smaller than full risk assessment
- Both quantitative and qualitative approaches
- Conduct a loss impact analysis.
- Necessary to define loss criteria quantitatively and qualitatively

Quantitative Loss Criteria
- Incurring financial loss from loss of revenue or capital expenditure
- Additional operational expenses incurred due to disruptive event
- Incurring financial loss from resolution of violated contract
- Incurring financial loss from regulatory compliance

Qualitative Loss Criteria
- Loss of competitive edge
- Loss of public confidence
- Incurring public embarrassment

Critical Support Areas must be defined:
- Telecommunications, data communications, Information Technology Areas
- Physical Infrastructure or plant facilities, transportation
- Accounting, Payroll, transaction processing, customer service, purchasing

Analyze The Compiled Information
- Documenting the process
- Identify Interdependencies
- Determine acceptable interruption period

Documentation and Recommendation
- Full documentation of all processes, procedures, analysis and results

Business Continuity Plan Development
- Use of information from BIA to create recovery strategy plan
- Map out strategy:
    - Defining the continuity strategy
    - Document the continuity strategy

Criticality Survey – helps to identify the most critical business functions

IT Department
- Ensures adequate backup and restoration process
- Ensures physical security of vital network and hardware components
- Ensuring sufficient logical security
- Ensuring adequate system administration

Defining the Continuity Strategy

Elements of Continuity Strategy
- **Computing** – needs to preserve hardware and software, communication lines, applications and data
- **Facilities** – needs to address use of buildings
- **People** – defined roles in implementing the strategy
- **Supplies and equipment** – paper, forms, HVAC, security equipment

Documenting the Continuity Strategy
- Creation of documentation

Plan Approval and Implementation
Last step plan is implemented
- Approval by Senior Management – must be able to make informed decisions in the event of a disaster
- Creating awareness – training and awareness enterprise wide
- Maintenance of the plan – plans get outdated quickly

Disaster Recovery Planning
- Comprehensive statement of actions to be taken before, during and after a disruptive event causes loss of Information Systems.
- Primary objective is to provide an alternate site and return to primary site in a minimal time frame

Goals and Objectives of DRP
- Provide an organized way to make decisions if a disruptive event occurs
- Reduce confusion and enhance the ability to deal with crisis
- Planning and development must occur before the disaster
- Objectives:
  - Protect the company from major computer services failure
  - Minimize the risk from delays in providing services
  - Guarantee reliability of standby systems through testing
  - Minimize decision making required by personnel during a disaster

- DRP assumes BIA has been done, now focusing on the steps needed to protect the business.

Data Processing Continuity Planning – planning for disaster and creating plans to cope with it
Data Recovery plan Maintenance – keeping plans up to date

Data Processing Continuity Planning
- Mutual Aid Agreements – reciprocal agreement
- Arrangement with another company with similar hardware or software configurations
- Agreement by both parties, assumes sufficient capacity in time of need (Big Assumption)
- Should only be considered if no other options, or perfect partner (i.e. subsidiary)
- **Advantages:**
  - Very little or no cost
  - If processing requirements are similar it may be workable
- **Disadvantages:**
  - Highly unlikely the capacity will exist
  - Severely limits responsiveness and support

Subscription Service
- Third party commercial services provide alternate backup and processing facilities
- Most common of the implementations.
- Three Basic Forms:
  - Hot Site
  - Warm Site
  - Cold Site

Hot Site
- Requires:
  - Fully configured facility with electrical power, Heating Ventilation and Air Conditioning (HVAC)
  - File and print servers and workstations
  - Applications are installed on the servers
  - Workstations are kept up to date

- Allows walk in with a data restoration and begin full operations in short time
- Remote journaling – mirroring transaction processing over high-speed connections may eliminate back up time.

- **Advantages:**
    - 24/7 availability
    - Exclusivity of use
    - Immediately available
    - Supports short and long term outages
- **Disadvantages:**
    - Most expensive
    - Requires constant maintenance of hardware, software, data and applications
    - Adds administrative overhead and can be a strain on resources
    - Service provider may oversell processing capabilities
    - Security of hot site, primary site security must be duplicated

Warm Site
Cross between hot and cold sites
- Facility with electrical power, Heating Ventilation and Air Conditioning (HVAC)
- File and print servers may not have workstations, software may not be installed
- External communications should be installed

- **Advantages:**
    - Cost – much less than hot
    - Location – since less control required sites can be more flexible
    - Resources – resource drain is much lower than hot site

Disadvantages:
- Difference in time required to be up and running

Cold Site
Least ready of all three, but most common
- Facility with electrical power, Heating Ventilation and Air Conditioning (HVAC)
- Ready for equipment but no computer hardware on site.
- Communications links may or may not be ready
- Not considered adequate because of length of time for recovery
- **Advantages:**
    - Cost

Disadvantages:
- False sense of security

Multiple Centers
- Processing spread over multiple centers, creating distributed redundancy. Can be in-house or through reciprocal agreement.
- Cost is contained, but same issues as Mutual Aid Agreements (reciprocal agreement)

Service Bureaus
- Contract with service bureau to provide all alternate backup processing.
- Advantage – quick response
- Disadvantage – cost, resource contention during disaster

Other alternatives:

Rolling mobile backup sites
- Vendor provides mobile services, mobile homes or flatbed trucks with power and HVAC sufficient for alternate processing. Considered Cold Site variation.

In-house or external supply of hardware replacements
- Vendors resupply hardware or internal stockpiling of critical components.
- Subscription service with vendor for overnight shipping
- May be OK for Warm site but not Hot site

Prefabricated Buildings
Use of prefabricated (mobile homes). Very cold site.

Transaction Redundancy Implementations
Fault tolerance and redundancy in Transaction processing

- **Electronic Vaulting** – transfer of backup date to off-site location. Batch process through communication lines
- **Remote Journaling** – parallel processing of transactions at remote site. Live data is posted as it occurs
- **Database Shadowing** – live processing of remote journaling but creates more redundancy by duplicating the database sets

Disaster Recovery Plan Maintenance
- Disaster Recovery Plans often get out of date
- Changes in technical infrastructure and company structure
- Plan maintenance must be employed from the outset
- Audit procedures should report regularly on the plan
- Version control on all plan copies

Testing of the Disaster Recovery Plan
- Testing must be conducted in an orderly, standardized fashion, executed on a regular basis
- No demonstrated recovery ability exists until it is tested
- Testing verifies the accuracy of the recovery procedures
- Testing prepares and trains personnel to execute during emergency
- Testing verifies the processing capability of the alternate backup site

Creating the Test Document
Test document should include:
- Test scenarios
- Reasons for the test
- Objectives of the test
- Type of tests
- Testing schedule
- Duration of the test
- Specific test steps
- Who will be the participants
- The task assignments of the test
- Resources and services required

- Test must not disrupt normal business functions
- Testing should start with easy areas to build skills and confidence
- Purpose is to find weaknesses, update and retest

The Five Disaster Recovery Plan Types
- Checklist
- Structured walk through
- Simulation
- Parallel
- Full-interruption

Checklist
- Preliminary step to real test, distribute plan for review by business unit managers

Structured Walk Through
- Business Unit Managers walk through the test plan. Each step is walked through and marked as performed.

Simulation
- All personnel with DR responsibilities will meet and go through a practice session
- Enacts recovery procedures but no alternate processing

Parallel
- Full test of recovery plan using all personnel. Primary processing does not stop. Ensures processing will run at alternate site. Most common type of recovery plan testing.

Full-interruption
- Disaster is replicated to the point of ceasing normal operations. Plan is implemented as if it were a disaster.
- Scary and can cause its own disaster, but best way to test completely

Disaster Recovery Procedures
Primary elements of the disaster recovery process
- Recovery team
- Salvage Team
- Normal Operations Team
- Other Recovery Issues

Recovery Team
- Implement the recovery procedures in a disaster
- Get critical functions operating at backup site
- Retrieval of materials from off-site storage, backups, workstations
- Installs critical systems and applications

Salvage Team
- Separate from recovery team
- Returns the primary site to normal operating conditions
- Safely clean, repair, salvage the primary processing facility

Normal Operations Team
- Task of Recovery Team, or another separate team
- Returning production from the alternate site to the primary site
- Disaster is not over until all operations have returned to their normal location and function.

Other Recovery Issues
- **Interfacing with external groups**
  - Municipal Emergency Groups, fire, police, ambulances, EMS.
  - Escalation and interaction should be included in the plan
- **Employee Relations**
  - Inherent responsibility to employees and their families
  - Salaries must continue
  - Insurance must be adequate
- **Fraud and crime**
  - Fraudsters try to capitalize on the disaster
  - Vandalism and looting may occur
- **Financial Disbursement**
  - Expense disbursement
  - Signed and authorized checks will be needed

- **Media Relations**
    - Unified response
    - Credible, trained, informed, spokesperson
    - Company should be accessible
    - Control dissemination of information

Under "Named Perils" form of Property Insurance: Burden of proof that particular loss is covered is on Insured

Maximum Tolerable Downtime (MTD): It is maximum delay businesses can tolerate and still remain viable

System reliability is increased by: A higher MTBF and a lower MTTR.

Valuable paper insurance coverage does not cover damage to: Money and Securities

A business continuity plan is an example of which of the following? : Corrective control

Under "All Risk" form of Property Insurance: Burden of proof that particular loss is not covered is on Insurer

A contingency plan should address: Residual risks

Business Continuity and Disaster Recovery Planning (Primarily) addresses the: Availability of the CIA triad

Domain 9 – Law, Investigation and Ethics

Covers computer crimes, preserving evidence and conducting basic investigations.

Many computer crimes go unreported – difficult to estimate.

Two Categories:
- Crimes against the computer
- Crimes using a computer

Most Common Crimes:
- Denial of Service (DoS)- hogging system resources to point of degraded service
- Theft or passwords
- Network Intrusions – unauthorized penetrations
- Emanation Eavesdropping – interception of computer terminal images through use of Radio Frequency (RF) Signals. U.S. Government developed Tempest to defeat this by shielding RF.
- Social Engineering – social skills to gain information
- Illegal Content of Material - porn
- Fraud – using computer to perpetuate crimes, i.e. auctions of non-existent merchandise
- Software Piracy – illegal copying
- Dumpster Diving – paper trails
- Malicious Code – viruses and Trojan Horses
- Spoofing of IP Addresses – inserting false IP to disguise original location
- Information Warfare – attacking infrastructure of a Nation, including military and power grid
- Espionage
- Destruction or alteration of information
- Use of readily available Attack Scripts – Script Kiddies, unskilled users
- Masquerading – pretending to be someone else
- Embezzlement – Illegally acquiring funds
- Data-Diddling – modification of data
- Terrorism

Examples of Crime –
- DDoS of Yahoo, Amazon and ZDNet in Feb. 2000
- Love Letter Worm in May of 2000
- Kaiser – transmissions of personal client information to unintended recipients in Aug. 2000
- Penetration of Microsoft, access to source code in Oct. 2000
- Mitnik's attacks against telephone companies 1989, broke into Tsutomo Shimomurs Corp in 1995 and was arrested
- Wisconsin medical records in 1982
- Morris internet worm DDoS Cornell Student in 1988
- Germans working for the KGB accessed US Classified Systems – The Cuckoo's Egg

Laws have been passed in many countries. International boundaries cause issues. Being addressed by United Nations, Interpol, European Union and the G8.

Technology outpaces Law
- Law enforcement relies on traditional laws against embezzlement, fraud, Denial of Service, wiretapping and digital currency to prosecute.

Many types of legal systems in the world
Common Law – United States, United Kingdom, Australia and Canada
- **Islamic Law**
- **Religious Law**
- **Civil Law** – France, Germany, Quebec

Common Law – United States
Three Branches of Government
Legislative – makes the statutory laws
Administrative – administrative laws
Judicial – common laws found in court decisions

Compilation of Statutory Law
Arranged in order of enactment or as statutory codes
In the U.S. held in Statutes at Large in the United States Code (U.S.C.)
Usually quoted "18 U.S.C § 1001 (1992)"
■ The Code Title Number
■ Abbreviation of the Code (U.S.C.)
■ Statutory section
■ Date of the edition

Title 18 of the 1992 Edition of the U.S.C. - contains Crimes and Criminal Procedures. Many computer crimes are prosecuted under this title.

US Computer Fraud and Abuse Act – addresses fraud using government computers can be found at 18 U.S.C. § 1030 (1986)

Other Titles Are:
Title 12 – Banks and Banking
Title 15 – Commerce and Trade
Title 26 – Internal Revenue Code
Title 49 - Transportation

Compilation of Administrative Law
Chronologically listed in administrative registers or by subject matter in administrative codes. Federal Register (Fed. Reg.) and Code of the Federal Register (C.F.R.)
Referenced "12 C.F.R. § 100.4 (1992)
■ The Title Number Federal Register (C.F.R.)
■ Abbreviation of the Code (C.F.R.)
■ Section number
■ Year of publication

Compilation of Common Law - common law from court decisions
■ Common law is compiled as Case Reporters in chronological order and Case Digests by Subject matter

Common Law System Categories – not to be confused with common law from court decisions
■ **Criminal Law** – Violates government laws for the protection of the people. Financial penalties and imprisonment
■ **Civil Law** – wrong inflicted upon an individual or organization results in damage or loss, no prison
■ **Administrative Law** – standards of performance and conduct, financial penalties and imprisonment

Intellectual Property Law
■ **Patent** – Provides owner legally enforceable right to exclude others for specified time (U.S. 17 years)
■ **Copyright** – Protects original works of authorship, can be used for software and databases
■ **Trade Secret** – Secures confidentiality of proprietary technical and business related information
  ■ Company must meet requirements:
    ■ Invested resources to develop the information
    ■ Valuable to the business
    ■ Valuable to competitor
    ■ Non-obvious information
■ **Trademark** – establishes word, name, symbol, color or sounds used to identify and distinguish goods

Information Privacy Laws
- Intent varies widely from country to country
- **European Union** - has developed more protective laws for individual privacy
  - Transfer of data from EU to US is prohibited unless equivalent protections are in place

EU Principles Include:
- Data collected in accordance with law
- Information cannot be disclosed without consent
- Records should be accurate and up to date
- Data should be used for the purpose it was collected
- Individuals entitled to report of information kept about them
- Transfer of data is prohibited unless equivalent protections are in place

Health Care Issues:
- Access controls do not provide sufficient granularity to implement least privilege rule
- Most off the shelf systems do not have adequate controls
- Systems must be accessible to outside parties
- Access to Internet creates potential problems
- Criminal and civil penalties can be imposed
- Public perception of large organizations misusing data

Health Care Should follow: (based on E.U. principles)
- Individual should have ability to monitor stored information about themselves, ability to correct information
- Data should be used for the purpose it was collected
- Organization should provide safeguards to ensure data is used for the purpose it was collected
- Existence of private information should not be kept secret

HIPAA –
U.S. Kennedy-Kassenbaum Health Insurance portability and Accountability Act. HIPAA effective August 21, 1996.
Addresses Health Care privacy in the U.S.
Still in draft form, required to be implemented soon.

Addresses:
- The rights of the individual has over information about them
- Procedures for the execution of such rights
- The uses and disclosures that should be authorized

Entity must have in place:
- **Standard Safe Guards** - must have appropriate administrative, technical and physical safeguards
- **Implementation of Standard Safe Guards** - A covered entity must protect health care information from intentional or unintentional disclosure

Electronic Monitoring
Keystroke monitoring, e-mail monitoring, surveillance cameras, badges and magnetic card keys all allow monitoring of individuals.
Key to monitoring: Must be done in a lawful manner in a consistent fashion

E-mail monitoring:
- Inform users that all e-mail is being monitored by displaying log-on banner
  - Banner should state: logging on to system consents user to being monitored. Unauthorized access is prohibited. Subject to prosecution.
- Ensure monitoring is uniformly applied
- Explain acceptable use
- Explain who can read e-mail and how long it is backed up
- No guarantee of privacy

Enticement vs. Entrapment
- Enticement occurs after individual has gained unlawful access to a system, then lured to an attractive area "honey pot" in order to provide time to identify the individual
- Entrapment encourages the commitment of a crime that the individual had no intention of committing

Computer Security, Privacy and Crime Laws:
- **1970 – US Fair Credit Reporting Act** – consumer reporting agencies
- **1970 - US Racketeer Influenced and Corrupt Organization Ace** – racketeers influencing business
- **1973 – US Code of Fair Information Practices** – personal record keeping
- **1974 – US Privacy Act** – applies to federal agencies
- **1980 Organization for Economic Cooperation and Development (OECD)** – data collection limitations
- **1984 – US Medical Computer Crime Act** – illegal alteration of computerized medical records
- **1984 – (Strengthened in 1986 and 1994) – First US Federal Computer Crime Law** – classified defense, felony for classified information
- **1986 (Amended 1996) – US Computer Fraud and Abuse Act** – clarified 1984 law, Added three laws:
    - use of federal interest computer to further intended fraud
    - altering or destroying information on federal interest computer that causes $1,000 in loss or medical treatment
    - Trafficking in computer passwords if it affects commerce or allows access to government computers
- **1986 Electronic Communications Privacy Act** – prohibits eavesdropping
- **1987 – Computer Security Act** – requires federal government to:
    - Provide security-related training
    - Identify sensitive systems
    - Develop security plan for sensitive systems
    - Developed Sensitive But Unclassified (SBU) designation
    - Split responsibility between National Institute of Standards and Technology (NIST) and National Security Agency (NSA)
        - NIST – commercial and SBU
        - NSA – cryptography and classified government and military applications
- **1990 United Kingdom Misuse Act** – defines computer related crimes
- **1991 US Federal Sentencing Guidelines** –
    - Unauthorized possession without the intent to profit is a crime
    - Address both individuals and organizations
    - Degree of punishment corresponds to level of due diligence
    - Invoke "prudent man" rule due care of Senior Officials – Civil Law
    - Place responsibility on Senior Management for prevention and detection programs up to $290 Million - Civil Law
- **1992 OECD – Guidelines to serve as Total Security Framework** – laws, policies, procedures, training
- **1994 – US Communications Assistance for Law Enforcement Act** – requires communications carriers to make wiretaps possible
- **1994 - Computer Abuse Amendments Act** –
    - Changed federal interest computer to a computer used in interstate commerce or communications
    - Covers viruses and worms
    - Includes intentional damage as well as reckless disregard
    - Limited imprisonment for unintentional damage to one year
    - Provides civil action for compensatory damages
- **1995 Council Directive Law on Data Protection for the European Union** – declares EU is similar to OECD
- **1996 – US Economic and Protection of Proprietary Information Act** – industrial and corporate espionage
- **1996 U.S. Kennedy-Kassenbaum Health Insurance portability and Accountability Act. HIPAA**

- **1996 National Information Infrastructure Protection Act** – amended the computer fraud and abuse act patterned after the OECD.
- **GAASSP** – Generally Accepted Systems Security Principles (Not laws but accepted principles of the OECD)
    - Computer security supports the business mission
    - Computer security is integral to sound management
    - Computer security should be cost effective
    - System Owners have responsibility outside of their organization
    - Computer security requires a comprehensive integrated approach
    - Computer security should be periodically reassessed
    - Computer security is constrained by societal factors

Pending Laws
- Uniform Electronic Transactions Act – applies the Federal Electronic Signatures act to the state level
- Uniform Computer Information Transactions Act – licensing terms on shrink wrapped software

Gramm-Leach-Bliley
Gramm-Leach-Bliley (PL 106-102) was signed into law on 12 November 1999. Title V of the law deals with Privacy. Title V Section 501 establishes policy for the **protection** of nonpublic personal information. Section 501 states, "It is the policy of the Congress that each financial institution has an affirmative and continuing obligation to respect the privacy of its customers and to protect the security and confidentiality of those customers' nonpublic personal information."

The law further states, financial regulatory agencies/authorities will "establish appropriate standards for the financial institutions subject to their jurisdiction relating to administrative, technical, and physical safeguards:
(1) to insure (sic) the security and confidentiality of customer records and information;
(2) to protect against any anticipated threats or hazards to the security or integrity of such records; and
(3) to protect against unauthorized access to or use of such records or information which could result in substantial harm or inconvenience to any customer."

Investigation
Also known as computer forensics – collecting information from and about computer systems that is admissible in a court of law.

Computer Forensic Issues
- Compressed timeframe for investigation
- Information is intangible
- Investigation may interfere with normal business operations
- May find difficulty in gathering evidence
- Co-mingling of live production data and evidence
- Experts are required
- Locations may be geographically in different jurisdictions
    - Differences in law and attitude
- **Many jurisdictions have expanded definitions of property to include electronic information**

Evidence
- Gathering, control and preservation are critical
- Subject to easy modification without a trace, must be carefully handled though its life cycle.
- Chain of Command - must be followed
- **Chain of Command components:**
    - Location of evidence
    - Time evidence obtained
    - Identification of individual who discovered evidence
    - Identification of individual who obtained evidence
    - Identification of individual who controlled/maintained possession of evidence

Evidence Life Cycle
- Discovery and recognition
- Protection
- Recording
- Collection
    - Collect all relevant storage media
    - Make image of hard disk before removing power
    - Print out screen
    - Avoid degaussing equipment
- Identification (tagging and marking)
- Preservation
    - Protect from magnetic erasure
    - Store in proper environment
- Transportation
- Presentation in court
- Return to evidence owner

Evidence Admissibility
- Evidence must meet stringent requirements.
- Must be **relevant, legally permissible, reliable, properly identified and preserved**
    - **Relevant** – must be related to the crime, shows crime has been committed
    - **Legally Permissible** – obtained in lawful manner
    - **Reliable** – not been tampered or modified
    - **Properly Identified** – identified without changing or damaging evidence
    - **Preservation** – not subject to damage or destruction
        - Make backups, write protect, take digital signatures of files or disk sectors

Types of Evidence
- Best Evidence – Original or primary evidence rather than a copy
- Secondary evidence – a copy of evidence, or description of contents
- Direct Evidence – proves or disproves a specific act based on witness testimony using five senses
- Conclusive Evidence – incontrovertible, overrides all evidence
- Opinions Two Types:
    - Expert – may offer opinion based on expertise and facts
    - Nonexpert – may testify only to the facts
- Circumstantial – inference on other information
- Hearsay – not based on first hand knowledge, not admissible in court, often computer generated reports fall under this rule.
- Exceptions to Hearsay Rule:
    - Made during the regular conduct of business with witnesses
    - Made by a person with knowledge of records
    - Made by person with knowledge
    - Made at or near time of occurrence of act
    - In the custody of the witness on regular basis

Searching and Seizing Computers
U.S. D.O.J. Computer Crime and Intellectual Property Sections (CCIPS) has issued the publication "Searching and Seizing Computers and Obtaining Evidence in Criminal Investigations".
Sites the following US Codes:
- 18 U.S.C. § 12510 - Definitions
- 18 U.S.C. § 1251 – interception and disclosure of wire, oral or electronic communications
- 18 U.S.C. § 2701 – unlawful access to stored communications
- 18 U.S.C. § 2702 – disclosure of contents
- 18 U.S.C. § 2703 – requirements for governmental access
- 18 U.S.C. § 2705 – delayed notice

- 18 U.S.C. § 2711 – definitions
- 18 U.S.C. § 2000aa – searches and seizures by government officers and employees in connection with the investigation of a crime

Export Issues with Technology
- In July of 2000 U.S. relaxed its encryption export policy to certain countries.
- American companies can export encryption to any end user.
- Eliminated third day of waiting period when exporting

Conducting the Investigation
- Corporate investigation should include Management, corporate security, Human Resources, legal department and other appropriate staff.
- May prompt retaliatory acts from the investigate, important to plan ahead
- Committee should be set up before hand to address the following issues:
    - Establishing liaison with law enforcement
    - Deciding when and if to bring in law enforcement (FBI and Secret Service)
    - Setting up means of reporting computer crimes
    - Establishing procedures for handling reports of computer crimes
    - Planning and conducting investigations
    - Involving senior management and corporate security, Human Resources, the legal dept.
    - Ensuring proper collection of evidence

- U.S. Federal Requirements requires crimes to be reported.
- U.S. government must obtain warrant to search for evidence under the 4th amendment. Must be probable cause.
- Private individuals **can** conduct a search without a warrant.
- **Exigent Circumstances Doctrine** – (Probable Cause) then do not need a warrant.

Good sources of evidence include:
- Telephone records
- Video cameras
- Audit trails
- System logs
- System backups
- Witnesses
- Results of surveillance
- E-mails

MOM
- Motive
- Opportunity
- Means

Interview:
- If interviewing do not give information away to suspect
- Questions should be scripted
- Don't use original documents in the interview

Liability
1991 US Federal Sentencing Guidelines
- Unauthorized possession without the intent to profit is a crime
- Address both individuals and organizations
- Degree of punishment corresponds to level of due diligence
- Invoke "prudent man" rule due care of Senior Officials – Civil Law
- Place responsibility on Senior Management for prevention and detection programs up to $290 Million

Due Care Requirements:
- Means to prevent computer resources from being used as a source of attack on another organization
  - Relates to proximate causation – part of a chain that results in negative consequence
- Backups
- Scans for malicious code
- Business Continuity and Disaster Recovery
- Local and remote access control
- Elimination of unauthorized insecure modems
- Security polices and procedures
  - Ensuing Confidentiality, Integrity and Availability
  - Assessing responsibilities to third parties
  - Established incident response capability

Downstream liabilities: When companies come together to work in an integrated manner, special care must be taken to ensure that each party promises to provide the necessary level of protection, liability and responsibility needed which should be clearly defined in the contracts that each party signs.

Due Care: Steps that are taken to show that a company has taken responsibility for the activities that take place within the corporation and have taken the necessary steps to help protect the company, its resources and employees.

Due Diligence: Continual activities that make sure the protection mechanisms are continually maintained and operational.

Prudent man rule: To perform duties that prudent people would exercise in similar circumstances.

Criteria for evaluating legal requirements:
C – cost of implementing the control
L – estimated loss from exploitation
If – C < L, then a legal liability exists.

Incident Handling should address:
- What constitutes an incident
- How should an incident be reported
- To who should an incident be reported
- When should management be informed of an incident
- What action should be taken if an incident occurs
- Who should handle the response to the incident
- How much damage was caused by the incident
- What data was damaged by the incident
- Are recovery procedures required
- What type of follow up or review is required
- Should additional safeguards be implemented

Establish a CIRT – Computer Incident Response Team

Ethics
Certified professionals are morally and legally held to a higher standard.
Should be included in organizational computing policy

ISC2 Code of Ethics:
CISSPs Shall:
1. Conduct themselves with highest standards of ethical, moral and legal behavior
2. Not commit any unlawful or unethical act that may impact the reputation of the profession
3. Appropriately report unlawful behavior
4. Support efforts to promote prudent information security measures

5. Provide competent service to their employers and clients; avoid conflicts of interest
6. Execute responsibilities with highest standards
7. Not misuse information in which they come into contact with during their duties

The Computer Ethics Institute Top Ten: (What is this **crap** doing in here?)
1. Not use a computer to harm others
2. Interfere with other's computer work
3. Snoop around other files
4. Use a computer to steal
5. Use a computer to bear false witness
6. Not copy or use proprietary software
7. Not use others computer without permission
8. Not appropriate others intellectual output
9. Think about social consequences of the programs you write
10. Ensure considerations and respect for others

Internet Activities Board (IAB)
"Internet Activity Should be treated as a privilege"
Unacceptable actions:
- Seeks to gain unauthorized access to resources of the Internet
- Disrupts intended use of the internet
- Wastes resources
- Compromises privacy of others
- Involves negligence in conduct of Internet Experiments

US Dept. Of Health, Education and Warfare
Fair information practices, individually identifiable information
- No personal record keeping on systems that are secret
- Way for person to find out what information is contained and how it is used
- Way for person to prevent information from being used for other purposes than originally intended
- Organizations must ensure reliability of data

Phone Phreakers
- **Blue boxing** - A device that simulates a tone that tricks the telephone company's system into thinking the user is authorized for long distance service, which enables him to make the call.
- **Red boxes** - Simulates the sound of coins being dropped into a payphone.
- **Black boxes** - Manipulates the line voltage to receive a toll-free call.

Domain 10 – Physical Security

Threats, Vulnerabilities and Countermeasures
- Goal is to protect resources including, personnel, the facility in which they work, data, equipment, support systems, and media.

Threats to Physical Security
Risks to Physical Security
- Interruptions in providing computer services – Availability
- Physical Damage – Availability
- Unauthorized disclosure of information – Confidentiality
- Loss of control over the system – Integrity
- Physical theft – Confidentiality, Availability, Integrity

Threats to Physical Security
- Emergencies
  - Fire and smoke
  - Building collapse
  - Utility loss
  - Water Damage
  - Toxic Materials
- Natural Disasters
  - Earth Quakes
  - Storm Damage
- Human Intervention
  - Sabotage
  - Vandalism
  - War
  - Strikes

- **Seven major sources of physical loss – from "Fighting Computer Crime"**
  1. Temperature – extreme variations in heat or cold
  2. Gases – war gases, commercial vapors, humidity, dry air, fuel vapors
  3. Liquids -- water and chemicals
  4. Organisms – viruses, bacteria, people, animals, insects
  5. Projectiles – meteorites, falling objects, cars, truck, bullets, rockets
  6. Movement – collapse, shearing, shaking, vibration, slides
  7. Energy Anomalies – electric surges, magnetism, static electricity, radio waves, micro waves

Controls for Physical Security
Two areas:
- Administrative
- Physical and Technical

Administrative Controls
- Benefits from the proper administrative steps
- Emergency procedures, personnel control, proper planning, policy implementation

Facility Requirements Planning – need for planning of security early on in construction
Choosing a Secure Site
- Visibility – what kind of neighbors, external markings, low visibility is the key
- Local Considerations – near hazards, high crime areas
- Natural Disaster – on a fault line, in a flood plain
- Transportation – excessive air or highway and road traffic
- Joint Tenancy – are environmental controls shared

- External Services – proximity of local emergency services

Designing a Secure Site
- **Walls** – acceptable fire rating, media rooms should have a high fire rating
- **Ceilings** – weight bearing and fire rating
- **Floors**:
  - **Slab** – Physical weight the concrete slab can bear and its fire rating
  - **Raised** – fire rating, electrical conductivity, non conducting surface material
- **Windows** – not acceptable in the data center, if so translucent and shatterproof
- **Doors** – must resist forcible entry, clear emergency exits, doors should open in an emergency (fail-soft)
- **Sprinkler System** – location and type of suppression system
- **Liquid and gas lines** – shutoff locations, water drains should be "positive" carry away from the building
- **Air Conditioning** – AC should have dedicated power circuits, Location of Emergency Power Off (EPO) switch, should provide outward positive air pressure to prevent contaminants
- **Electrical Requirements** – backup alternate power, dedicated circuits, access controls over panels

Facility Security Management
Audit Trails and Emergency Procedures

Audit Trails – log of events, systems may have many audit logs each capturing specific information
- Access logs should contain:
  - Date and Time Access attempted
  - Whether the attempt was successful or not
  - Where was access granted (which door)
  - Who attempted Access
  - Who modified access privileges at the supervisor level
- Some trails can send alerts
- Audit Trails are detective not preventative

Emergency Procedures
Clearly documented, readily accessible and updated periodically
- Should include:
  - Emergency Shutdown procedures
  - Evacuation procedures
  - Employee training, awareness and periodic drills
  - Periodic System tests

Administrative Personnel Controls
Implemented commonly by the HR department during hiring and firing
- Pre-employment screening
  - Employment references, educational history
  - Background checks, credit
- On going employee checks
  - Security clearances – if required
  - Ongoing evaluations and reviews
- Post-employment
  - Exit interview
  - Removal of network access
  - Return of computer inventory, laptops

Environmental and Life Safety
Sustain computer and personnel operating environment
Three focus areas:
- Electrical power

- Fire detection and suppression
- Heating Ventilation and Air Conditioning

Electrical power

Electrical Power Terminology	Description
Fault	Momentary loss of power
Blackout	Complete loss of power
Sag	Momentary low voltage
Brownout	Prolonged low voltage
Spike	Momentary high voltage
Surge	Prolonged high voltage
Inrush	Initial surge of power
Noise	Steady interference
Transient	Short duration of line noise
Clean	Non-fluctuating power
Ground	One wire is grounded

Clean steady power supply - Most common threats are noise, brown outs, and humidity

Noise - Presence of electrical radiation in the system interferes with distribution of clean power

Several Types of Noise:
- Most common is Electromagnetic Interference (EMI) and Radio Frequency Interference (RFI)
- EMI is caused by the generation of radiation due to charge differences between the hot, neutral and ground wires.
- Two common types of Electromagnetic Interference - EMI are:
  - **Common Mode noise** - the generation of radiation due to charge differences between the hot and ground wires
  - **Traverse Mode Noise:** the generation of radiation due to charge differences between the hot and neutral wires

- Radio Frequency Interference (RFI) is generated by the components of an electrical system, can damage equipment

Protective measures for noise:
- Power Line Conditioning
- Proper Grounding
- Cable shielding
- Limiting exposure to magnets, fluorescent lights, motors and space heaters

Brownouts
Brownout is a prolonged drop in supplied usable voltage; can do serious damage to sensitive equipment
- American National Standards Institute allows:
  - 8% drop between building meter and the power source
  - 3.5% drop from the meter to the wall
- Surges and spikes as power comes back on line can also cause problems.
- Surge suppressors should protect all equipment and critical components require UPS.

Humidity
- The ideal Operating Range is between 40 to 60 percent.
- High humidity above 60% can cause condensation on parts. Also can cause corrosion of components
  - Silver plating goes to copper circuits impeding the electrical efficiency
- Low humidity less than 40% increase static electricity
- A static charge of 4,000 volts is possible under normal humidity on a hard wood floor

■ Charges up to 20,000 volts or more are possible under very low humidity with non-static free carpeting

Static Charge Volts	Damage
40	Sensitive circuits
1,000	Scramble monitor display
1,500	Disk drive data loss
2,000	System shutdown
4,000	Printer jam
17,000	Permanent chip damage

Control to prevent Static Electricity
■ Anti-static sprays where possible
■ Anti static flooring
■ Proper grounding
■ Anti-static tables
■ HVAC should maintain proper humidity levels

Fire Detection and Suppression

Three elements to sustain fire:
■ Oxygen
■ Heat - temperature
■ Fuel

Class	Description	Suppression Medium
A	Common combustibles	Water or soda acid
B	Liquid	CO2, soda acid, Halon
C	Electrical	CO2 or Halon
D	Combustible metals	Dry powder

■ **Water** – suppresses temperature required to sustain fire
■ **Soda Acid** – suppressed the fuel
■ **CO2** – Suppresses the oxygen
■ **Halon** – suppresses through chemical reaction that kills the fire

Fire Detectors
■ Heat sensing – detects one of two things:
　■ Temperature reaches specified level (less false positives)
　■ Temperature rises quickly
■ Flame Actuated – fairly expensive
　■ Sense infrared energy of flame or pulsation of the flame
■ Smoke Actuated – two types
　■ Photoelectric devices triggered by variation in light hitting photoelectric cells
　■ Radioactive device goes off when ionization current is created by radioactive reaction to smoke

Fire Extinguishing Systems
Wet Pipe
■ Sprinkler always contain water
■ At 165 ° F - fusible link in nozzle melts
■ Most reliable
■ Subject to leaking and freezing

Dry Pipe
■ No water standing in the pipe
■ Air is blown out and water is released

- Time delay can allow systems to power down

Deluge
- Dry pipe system
- Large Volume of Water
- Not good for computer equipment

Preaction
- Most recommended for computer room
- Combines wet and dry
- Charges pipe when heat is detected
- Releases water when - fusible link in nozzle melts

Gas Discharge
Pressurized inert gas released through raised floor
- Carbon Dioxide CO2
- Halon 1211 – does not require sophisticated pressurization
- Halon 1301 - requires sophisticated pressurization
- FM –200 is now most common Halon replacement

Carbon Dioxide CO2
- Colorless and odorless gas
- Removes oxygen and can be lethal if all oxygen is removed
- Used in unmanned facilities
- If used in manned system alarm must allow adequate time to evacuate or cancel

Portable Extinguishers should be located:
- Commonly located exits
- Clearly marked with their fire types
- Checked regularly

Halon – at one time was considered perfect suppression medium
- The two Types
  - Halon 1211 – liquid streaming agent used in portable extinguishers
  - Halon 1301 – gaseous agent used in fixed total flooding
- Not harmful to equipment
- Mixes thoroughly with air
- Spreads extremely fast
- **Problems:**
  - Can not be breathed safely in concentrations greater than 10%
  - Fires greater than 900° F it degrades to toxic chemicals Hydrogen Fluoride, Hydrogen Bromide and Bromine
  - Must allow adequate time to evacuate or cancel
  - Ozone depleting due to use of CFCs. Very high ozone depleting potential
- No new Halon 1301 installations allowed
- Existing encouraged to replace
- Federal law prohibits production of Halon
- Halon 1211 is being replaced
- Halon 1301 is being banked for future use

Common EPA replacements:
- FM-200
- CEA-410
- NAF-S-III
- FE-13
- Argon

- Inergen
- Low Pressure Water Mists

Contamination and Damage
- Smoke
- Water
- Heat
- Suppression Medium

Temperature Damage Points
- Computer Hardware - 175° F
- Magnetic Storage - 100° F
- Paper Products - 350° F

Heating Ventilation and Air Conditioning
- Designate who is responsible
- Clear escalation step in case of problems

Physical Technical Controls
Physical site security
- Guards
- Dogs
- Fencing
- Lighting
- Locks
- CCTV

Guards
- Can make judgments and adjust to rapidly changing conditions
- Provide deterrent capability
- Response and control
- Reception and escort
- Especially useful in personnel safety issues
- Drawbacks:
  - Availability – human intervention
  - Reliability – pre-employment screening not foolproof
  - Training – subject to social engineering, not always up to date
  - Cost – expensive

Dogs
- Loyal and reliable
- Keen senses
- Especially useful in Perimeter control
- Drawbacks:
  - Cost – expensive
  - Insurance – liability

Fencing
- Primary means of boundary control

Height	Protection
3' to 4' (1 meter)	Deters casual trespasser
6' to 7' (2 meters)	Too hard to climb easily
8' with 3 strands of barbed wire (2.4 meters)	Deters intruders

Mantrap — physical access control routed though a set of double doors that may be monitored by a guard

Lighting
- Lighting types – floodlights, street lights, and searchlights
- 8 feet high with 2 foot candle

Locks
- Two Types Preset and Programmable
  - **Preset Locks** – Typical Door Locks, must remove lock to change key
  - **Programmable** – Mechanical or electronic, dial combination lock

Cipher lock - Keypad, numbers change randomly

Closed Circuit Television
- Visual surveillance
- Record for analysis
- Photographic or Electronic
- Monitoring - preventative control
- Recording - detective control

Facility Access Control Devices
- Security Access Cards
- Two Types:
  - Photo image – dumb
  - Digitally Encoded – smart

Photo Image Cards
- Simple ID cards
- Require decision by guards

Digitally Encoded Cards
- Contain chips or magnetic stripes
- Card reader makes decisions as to access
- Can provide logging of activity
- Multi level access groupings
- Smart Card - ATM Card may require PIN
- Smart Card may be coupled with a token

Wireless Proximity Readers
- Does not require physically inserting the card
- Card reader senses the card
- Two Types:
  - User Activated – transmits keystroke sequence to a wireless keypad reader
  - System Sensing – senses card
    - Passive Devices – card contains no battery, senses electromagnetic field of reader and transmits frequency using power of reader
    - Field Powered Devices – contain active electronics on the card
    - Transponders - Both card and reader contain active electronics, transmitter, battery
    - Reader sends signal, card sends signal back

Card Types

Type of Card	Description
Photo ID	Facial photograph
Optical coded	Laser burned lattice of digital dots
Electric circuit	Printed chip on the card
Magnetic stripe	Stripe of magnetic material
Magnetic strip	Rows of copper strings
Passive electronic	Electrically-tuned circuitry read by RF
Active electronic	Badge transmits encoded electronics

Biometric Devices
- Are physical access devices

Intrusion Detection Alarms
- Identifying attempts to access a building
- Two most common types:
  - Photoelectric sensors
  - dry contact switches

Photoelectric sensors
- Receive beam of light from tight emitter
- Can be visible light, white light or infrared
- Alarm sounds if beam is broken
- Can be avoided if seen
- Invisible Infrared is often used
- Employing substitute light source can fool sensor

Dry Contact Switches
- Most common
- Metallic foil tape on windows and doors
- Easy and cheap

Motion Detectors
Wave Pattern
- Generate frequency wave pattern
- Sound alarm if disturbed
- Can be low frequency, ultrasonic, or microwave

Capacitance
- Monitor electrical field surrounding object
- Spot protections within a few inches of the object
- Not for entire room
- Penetration of field changes capacitance

Audio Detectors
- Passive, no generation of fields
- Simply monitor room for abnormal noise
- High number of false positives

Alarm Systems
Local Alarm Systems
- Rings an audible signal
- Must be protected from tampering

- Audible for at least 400 ft
- Requires guards to respond locally

Central Alarm Systems
- Private security firms
- Central station
- Offer CCTV monitoring
- Reporting
- Commonly 10 minutes or less travel time

Proprietary Alarm Systems
- Similar to central
- The company owns monitoring
- Like local but with features of the central system

Auxiliary Station Systems
- Any of the previous three may have auxiliary alarms ring at the fire or police station.
- Need permission from local authorities

Other Requirements:
Line Supervision
- Line is monitored to prevent tampering to subvert the alarm system.

Power Supplies
- Alarms should have backup power for a minimum of 24 hours

Computer Inventory Control
- Control of equipment from theft
- PC Control and laptop control

PC Control
- Cable locks – anchor the PC to the desk
- Port Controls – secure data ports (i.e. floppy drive) or serial or data ports and prevent their use
- Switch Controls – cover for on/off switch which prevent user from switching off file servers
- Peripheral switch controls – lockable switches prevent keyboard from being used
- Electronic Security Boards – inserted into a PC slot require password to boot, also included in BIOS

Laptop Control
- Encrypt the drive

Media Storage
- Proper disposal

Require storage, destruction or reuse:
- Data backups
- CDs
- Diskettes
- Hard Drives
- Paper printout

Common Storage areas:
- On-Site – areas within the facility
- Off-site – areas outside the facility, data backup service
  - Examine vendor security

Data Destruction and Reuse
- Must reformat **seven times** according to TCSEC Orange Book standards
- Shredders should crosscut
- Military will burn reports

Object Reuse
- Clearing – overwriting data media to be reused in same environment
- Purging – degaussing or overwriting to be used in another environment
- Destruction – completely destroying

Common Problems
- Erasing just deletes file header not data
- Damaged sectors may not be over written
- Rewriting may not write over all data areas, (slack space)
- Degauser equipment failure
- Inadequate number of formats

66432816R00057